Aspen Health Law Center Current Issues

EMPLOYEE BENEFITS

A Guide for Health Care Professionals

Aspen Health Law Center Current Issues

Managed Care: State Regulation

Health Care Fraud and Abuse

Physicians as Employees

Employment Discrimination in
the Health Care Industry

Employee Benefits:
A Guide for Health Care Professionals

Aspen Health Law Center
Current Issues

Employee Benefits

A Guide for Health Care Professionals

Aspen Health Law Center

Deborah Rosenbloom, Esq.

AN ASPEN PUBLICATION®
Aspen Publishers, Inc.
Gaithersburg, Maryland
1998

This publication is designed to provide accurate and authoritative information in regard to the Subject Matter covered. It is sold with the understanding that the publisher is not engaged in rendering legal, accounting, or other professional service. If legal advice or other expert assistance is required, the service of a competent professional person should be sought. (From a Declaration of Principles jointly adopted by a Committee of the American Bar Association and a Committee of Publishers and Associations.)

Library of Congress Cataloging-in-Publication Data
Employee benefits : a guide for health care professionals / Aspen Health Law Center, Deborah Rosenbloom.
p. cm. — (Aspen Health Law Center current issues)
Includes bibliographical references and index.
ISBN 0-8342-1158-0 (pbk.)
1. Insurance, Health—Law and legislation—United States. 2. Employee fringe benefits—Law and legislation—United States. I. Rosenbloom, Deborah. II. Aspen Health Law Center. III. Series.
KF3515.E48 1998
344.7301'255—dc21
98-9617
CIP

Orders: (800) 638-8437
Customer Service: (800) 234-1660

Editorial Services: Brian MacDonald
Library of Congress Catalog Card Number: 98-9617
ISBN: 0-8342-1158-0

Printed in the United States of America

1 2 3 4 5

Table of Contents

Preface

This book, *Employee Benefits: A Guide for Health Care Professionals*, is part of a collection of reference products addressing issues of current interest in the field of health care law. These products are designed to provide up-to-date, easy-to-retrieve information on a variety of topics selected on the basis of their relevance to late-breaking developments in the health care industry. The subjects covered in the inaugural group of products include *Managed Care: State Regulation, Health Care Fraud and Abuse, Physicians as Employees*, and *Employment Discrimination in the Health Care Industry*. Other topics will be added to this legal reference series as the need arises.

The books are designed to provide practical overviews of the principal legal issues relating to each topic. They are extensively footnoted, and a Table of Contents and Index provide easy access to the information. Most of the products also offer a selection of support documents, including statutory text, model contract language, and administrative rulings and guidance.

The series is compiled by the attorneys and editors on staff at the Health Law Center of Aspen Publishers, who contributed to developing these products through their writing and research efforts. We hope that these products, either separately or as a group, will meet the busy health care professional's ongoing need for information in the rapidly evolving field of health care law.

INTRODUCTION

Benefits personnel administer an array of complex functions. Their many tasks include managing benefits programs; processing retirements; managing unemployment compensation; maintaining personnel data and records; complying with federal and state regulations; providing forms to employees; developing methods to process documents; administering health and welfare programs; evaluating, designing, and implementing new programs; managing relationships with employees and vendors; ensuring legal compliance; processing payments to vendors; conducting benefits orientation and coordinating Consolidated Omnibus Budget Reconciliation Act (COBRA) administration; and ensuring employee job satisfaction and job commitment, which will lead to high productivity.

New challenges for the human resource administrator include management of cultural diversity, employee-employer communication, morale issues due to downsizing, corporate mergers and acquisitions, budget cuts, and help for employees in dealing with the stresses of their lives.

The roles of benefits personnel include critical communications with employees. Not only does the law require that notices be sent out informing employees of their benefits availability and their rights, communication is essential to the proper utilization of a benefits program. Posting information on the company's web site via the Internet or using a company intranet service is an excellent way to inform employees of their benefits choices. The information is easily updated and accessible. In fact, providing Internet or Intranet services as a way to reenroll in benefit plans can prove to be a cost- and time-saving method.

Benefits cover a large range of possibilities, and the decision of what to offer can reflect the concerns of the health care organization and its commitment to its employees. Benefits are expensive, and the benefits administrator must determine which benefits will be available to employees based on concern for cost and keeping in mind that a good benefits package can serve as a recruiting tool to hire and to increase commitment to the health care employer. As the 9th Circuit stated: "Few . . .

[employee benefits] are mere gratuities or a result of unadulterated altruism. Most are for services rendered or for the purpose of inducing the further rendering of services. They help to guarantee a competent and happy labor force."[1]

The high cost of the benefits provided by the employer should be communicated to employees in order to increase their appreciation. Some benefits are required by federal law and are given to employees automatically. They include the Federal Unemployment Tax Act (FUTA), Federal Insurance Contributors Act (FICA), and workers' compensation insurance. These benefits are costly to the employer and are taken for granted by the employee. Most benefits are discretionary with the employer. Discretionary benefits include dental; orthodontic; prescription drug plan; vision; hearing; wellness and preventive services; long-term care; disability; term and permanent group life insurance; dependent care programs, including elder care and day care for young children; family and medical leave programs; vacation time and leave time; sick time; personal days; flextime; employee meals paid for by organization; discounts on goods and services; group legal services plans; educational assistance programs; financial planning; and retirement plans, including profit sharing, 401(k) plans, employee stock ownership plans, individual retirement accounts (IRAs), simplified employee pensions (SEPs), Keogh plans, and executive retirement plans.

There are many issues for the health care resource administrator to be aware of when supervising plan administrators. Plan administrators should be able to develop creative employee benefits packages attractive to both the employer and employee. These packages should be designed to reflect the employer's concerns and commitments. The plan administrator must produce employee benefit plan material in a clear, concise way that complies with the applicable laws. Government reporting and compliance are critical aspects of the job. The health care benefits personnel must be careful not to step into the role of fiduciary when administering benefits plans. Fiduciaries are liable for failure to perform their duties, and benefits personnel are better off leaving these discretionary responsibilities to plan administrators. Fiduciary responsibilities include asset allocation, coordination with trust accountants, investment services, and investment policy.

Among the decisions the health care benefits administrator must make are which employees will be eligible for which benefits, keeping in mind the nondiscrimination rules applicable to many benefits. A recent case[2] emphasized the importance of including all employees who meet the minimum eligibility standards in benefits packages. Workers had been hired as "independent contractors." The Internal Revenue Service (IRS) found that they were indeed employees based on the facts of their employment situation. The workers were fully integrated into the work force, they worked the same core hours as employees, they worked on site, had admittance card-keys, and used the office equipment and supplies. However, they were paid through accounts receivable and not through payroll. The company did not withhold income or pay FICA taxes. The workers sued to be permitted to participate in benefits. Administrators should be aware of this decision and be certain that so called "independent contractors" are not actually employees and therefore entitled to benefits.

DISCRIMINATION RULES

Pension plans and welfare benefit plans, including qualified retirement plans, group legal services plans, 401(k) plans, health plans, and cafeteria plans, are subject to nondiscrimination rules. The nondiscrimination rules are complex, but the health care benefits specialist should be on the lookout for plans favoring highly compensated employees. Nondiscrimination testing is best understood if broken down into two components: eligibility and benefits. Eligibility tests the percentage of employees who are eligible to participate in an offered benefit. The benefits component examines the percentage of participants who actually benefit from the plan. The term *highly compensated employee* generally refers to an employee who receives $80,000 or more in compensation (as adjusted), is a 5 percent owner, or earns more than $50,000 and is in the highest compensated group of employees or is an officer and receives more than half of the defined benefit limitation.[3]

Self-insured health benefits plans use the "highly paid individual" as the benchmark for discrimination testing. Such an individual is one of the five highest paid officers, owns more than 10 percent of the employer's stock, or is in the top quarter of the highest paid employees. Discrimination testing excludes employees who have not completed three years of service; employees who are not yet 25 years old; part-time or seasonal employees; employees who are included in the unit of employees covered by a collective bargaining agreement covering health and accident benefits but who are not plan participants; and nonresident aliens.[4]

EMPLOYEE RETIREMENT INCOME SECURITY ACT

The Employee Retirement Income Security Act (ERISA) is a comprehensive federal statute governing both pension and nonpension plans, such as employee welfare benefits plans.[5] "The statute imposes participation, funding, and vesting requirements on pension plans. It also sets various uniform standards, including rules concerning reporting, disclosure, and fiduciary responsibility, for both pension and welfare plans."[6] The statute provides in pertinent part the following: "the terms *employee welfare benefit plan* and *welfare plan* mean any plan, fund, or program established or maintained by an employer or by an employee organization, or by both, to the extent that such plan, fund, or program was established or is maintained for the purpose of providing for its participants or their beneficiaries, through the purchase of insurance or otherwise, (A) medical, surgical, or hospital care or benefits, or benefits in the event of sickness, accident, disability, death, or unemployment, or vacation benefits, apprenticeship, or other training programs, or day care centers,[7] scholarship funds, or prepaid legal services."[8] Benefits given to laid-off employees such as Supplemental Unemployment Benefits (SUB) and Guaranteed Income Stream (GIS) are included in the definition.[9] Whether or not a particular set of insurance arrangements constitute an employee welfare benefit plan is a question of fact determined by established legal standards.[10] An employee welfare benefit plan does not include a group or group-type insurance program offered by an insurer to employees or members of an employee organization, under which any of the following apply:

1. No contributions are made by an employer or employee organization.
2. Participation in the program is completely voluntary for employees or members.
3. The sole functions of the employer or employee organization with respect to the program are, without endorsing the program, to permit the insurer to publicize the program to employees or members, to collect premiums through payroll deductions or dues checkoffs and to remit them to the insurer.
4. The employer or employee organization receives no consideration in the form of cash or otherwise in connection with the program, other than reasonable compensation, excluding any profit, for administrative services actually rendered in connection with payroll deductions or dues checkoffs.[11]

An ERISA plan is not established if the employer does not do more than purchase insurance for the employees without further involvement, such as either directly or indirectly assuming ownership, or controlling, administering, or assuming responsibility for the plan.[12] An ERISA plan is not established if the sole function of the employer is to permit the insurance company to publicize the program, to collect premiums through payroll or dues checkoff, and to remit the money to the insurer. However, where the employer distributed the booklet in its name, encouraging the employees to give it careful consideration, and employed a full-time employee benefits administrator who accepted claim forms and submitted them, the particular Department of Labor (DOL) regulations did not exclude the plan from ERISA.[13]

Summary Plan Descriptions

Summary plan descriptions (SPDs) are required for ERISA pension and welfare plans. This section will discuss generally the summary plan requirements for any ERISA pension or welfare plan offered by a health care organization to its employees. An SPD is a legally binding document containing information about the plan and the rights and obligations of a participant and a beneficiary that is written in simple, accessible language.[14] A notice that assistance is available to explain the SPD must be given where a proportion of the employees do not read English and do read the same foreign language.[15] Each plan participant and each plan beneficiary must be given a copy of the SPD within 90 days of either joining the plan or receiving benefits or within 120 days after the plan first becomes subject to ERISA's reporting and disclosure requirements.[16] However, failure to distribute an SPD does not entitle an employee to vested benefits.[17]

The SPD must contain specific information to comply with Federal law.[18] The health care administrator should use the following checklist to be sure the SPD complies with the law:

- the name and type of the plan's administration, such as control administration or insurer administration
- the name and address of the organization through which benefits are provided
- effective for plan years beginning on or after June 30, 1997, the following information is also required: If an insurance company, insurance service, or insurance organization (including a health maintenance organization [HMO]) is responsible in whole or in part for the financing or administration of a group health plan, the SPD must include its name and address, whether and to what extent benefits are guaranteed under a contract or policy of insurance, and the nature of the administrative services provided by the entity.
- the name and address of the plan's administrator
- the date the plan year ends
- the plan's name and plan number
- the employer's name and address if it is a single employer plan
- employer identification number (EIN) assigned by the IRS to the employer

- type of plan, for example, for pension plans, defined benefit, money purchase, profit sharing, and so forth, and for welfare plans, hospitalization, disability, prepaid legal service, and so forth. Note that after January 1, 1998, notice that maternity benefits are available must be stated in the SPD.
- the sources of contributions to the plan—for example, employer, employee organization, employees—and the method by which the amount of contribution is calculated; defined benefit pension plans may state without further explanation that the contribution is actuarially determined
- the name and address of the person designated as agent for service of legal process if the agent is not the administrator
- the names, titles, and addresses of all trustees if different from the administrator

If the plan was made pursuant to a collective bargaining agreement, the following apply:

- the names and addresses of the association, committee, board of trustees, parent or employer of a group of employers that contributes to the same plan or other similar representative of the parties
- a statement that a complete list of the employers and employee organizations sponsoring the plan may be obtained by the participants and the eligible beneficiaries upon written request to the plan administrator and is available for examination by participants and beneficiaries
- a statement that, upon written request, participants and beneficiaries may receive information as to whether a particular employer or employee organization is a sponsor of the plan and the sponsor's address

If the plan is established or maintained by two or more employers, the following apply:

- the name and address of the association, committee, joint board of trustees, parent or most significant employer of a group of employers all of which contribute to the same plan, or other similar representative of the parties who established or maintain the plan

- relevant collective bargaining provisions
- eligibility requirements for participation and benefits, such as age and years of service
- provisions for nonforfeitable pension benefits
- the circumstances that could result in disqualification, ineligibility, or denial or loss of the benefits (For employee welfare benefit plans that provide extensive schedules of benefits, only a general description is required *if* reference is made to detailed schedules of benefits that are available without cost to any participant or beneficiary requesting a copy)[19]

For an employee pension benefit plan, the following information is needed:

- the plan's normal retirement age and any other conditions that must be met before a participant will be eligible to receive benefits
- a statement describing joint and survivor benefits, including any election requirements
- a statement as to whether or not the benefits are insured, and, if not, why not; if the benefits of the plan are insured, then notice of the protections given by the Pension Benefit Guaranty Corporation (PBGC)
- the PBGC protects participants in a terminated pension plan. Certain procedures must be followed when terminating a pension plan. Notice of the intent to terminate must be provided by the plan sponsors to each affected party, and information must be given to the PBGC.[20] An attempt must be made to locate missing plan participants before transferring responsibility for payment to the PBGC. This applies both to standard terminations and to distress terminations (where the fund does not have enough funds).[21]
- a description and explanation of the plan provisions for determining years of service for eligibility to participate, vesting rules, and breaks in service
- a description and explanation of the number of years required for participation for benefit accrual, including the

service required to accrue full benefits and the way in which accrual of benefits is prorated for employees who do not complete a full year of employment

For an employee pension benefit plan that will use the "cut-back" rule[22] to make retroactive changes in the vesting or accrual provisions described in the summary plan description, the following will be needed:

- a statement that certain provisions of the plan are subject to amendment that directly or indirectly modifies certain plan rights and benefits
- the nature of those modifications
- the identification by reference of those plan provisions
- the identification by reference of the portions of the SPD where they are described; this may be either printed within the text of the summary plan description or on a separate sheet and disclosed together with the SPD.

The DOL office where plan participants can get further information about their rights must be included in health coverage plans pursuant to the Health Insurance Portability and Accountability Act (HIPAA) amendments.[23] Items that are not applicable to the plan are not required to be included. The statement may contain extra explanatory and descriptive provisions. However, the style and format of the statement cannot mislead, misinform, or fail to inform the participants and beneficiaries. All information must be written in a manner calculated to be understood by the average plan participant, taking into account factors such as the level of comprehension and education of typical participants. Inaccurate, incomprehensible, or misleading explanatory material does not meet these requirements. The statement of ERISA rights (the model statement or a statement prepared by the plan), must appear as one consolidated statement. The SPD may state that the statement of ERISA rights is required by Federal law and regulation.

The SPD should also contain a disclaimer putting participants and beneficiaries on notice that the plan itself is the controlling document. While this disclaimer will not necessarily protect the plan administrator or the plan's assets from lawsuits based on discrepancy between the SPD and the plan, it does serve to put participants and beneficiaries on notice. If there is a discrepancy between the plan document and the SPD, the SPD controls.[24] The issue of whether reliance on a faulty plan document is a prerequisite to an ERISA recovery is not resolved.[25] However, at least one circuit has held repeatedly that erroneous information by itself without a showing of bad faith, active concealment, or detrimental reliance does not state a cause of action under ERISA.[26] All or substantially all of the required information must be in the document in order for it to be an SPD.[27] A record-keeping booklet containing crucial information explaining benefits and circumstances that would disqualify a participant from securing benefits was held to be an SPD,[28] but a document was not an SPD where it instructed the employees to refer to the SPD, lacked most of the categories of required information, was perfunctory, and was an updated version of an early brochure that was not an SPD.[29]

Participants are also entitled to request and receive a statement of accrued benefits, the plan instrument, the plan's latest annual report, the trust agreement, and any document under which the plan is established.[30] Penalties may be assessed against the plan administrator for failure to provide these documents.[31]

Amendments to Plan

Participants and beneficiaries are notified of material changes to the plan or its administration by the Summary of Material Modifications (SMM). The SMM is distributed within 60 days of the adoption of a modification or change that is a material reduction in covered services or benefits.[32]

Examples of "reductions in covered services or benefits" include any plan modification or change that eliminates benefits payable under the plan; reduces benefits payable under the plan, including a reduction that occurs as a result of a change in formulas, methodologies, or schedules that serve as the basis for making benefit determinations; increases deductibles, co-payments, or other amounts to be paid by a participant or beneficiary; reduces the service area covered by an HMO; or establishes new conditions or requirements (e.g., preauthorization requirements) to obtain services or benefits under the plan.[33] An SMM is distributed within 210 days of the close of the plan year in which any other type of material modification is adopted.[34]

Preemption

ERISA is designed to provide uniformity of benefit plans for the protection of plan participants.[35] Therefore, it broadly "overrides" or "preempts" all state laws that "relate to any employee benefit plan."[36] This includes both state common law and statutory claims.[37] ERISA is concerned with the administration of benefits and not with the precise design of benefits plans.[38] The types of laws preempted by ERISA have been divided into four categories of laws relating to employee benefits plans:

1. laws regulating types of benefits or the terms of ERISA plans
2. laws creating reporting, disclosure, funding, or vesting for ERISA plans
3. rules for calculating benefits to be paid out
4. laws and common law rules providing remedies for misconduct growing out of ERISA administration[39]

A statute requiring hospitals to collect surcharges from patients insured by a commercial insurer and HMOs but not from patients insured by Blue Cross/Blue Shield was not preempted by ERISA. The surcharge provisions did not relate to employee benefits. They left the plan administrators where they would have been in any case—with the responsibility to choose the best overall coverage for the money. The surcharge provisions did not require the plan administrators to deal with only one insurer or to insure against the entire category of illnesses the plan might otherwise not choose to cover.[40] However, ERISA did preempt Maryland insurance regulations that fixed the minimum attachment point for stop-loss insurance policies issued to self-funded employee benefits plans covered by ERISA. The regulations were designed to prevent insurers and self-funded employment benefit plans from depriving participants and beneficiaries of state mandated health benefits. The plans contained substantially fewer benefits than the mandated ones, and the court found that the statute sought to regulate coverage of employee benefit plans.[41] Courts routinely find that claims that arose from the manner in which benefits were administered or that were premised on the type or extent of benefits promised or provided are preempted.[42] However, the alleged negligent misrepresentation of the scope of coverage of an employee benefit plan did not have a sufficient connection to ERISA and was not preempted.[43]

Fiduciary Issues

Generally, employers do not owe fiduciary duties to plan beneficiaries under ERISA.[44] Employers function as conduits collecting forms and disseminating information about the available benefits. A health care organization, however, can step into the role of fiduciary if it chooses to act as both employer and plan administrator. At this point, ERISA fiduciary duties regarding plan administration will attach.[45] The health care administrator should be careful not to overstep the lines drawn by courts so as to prevent being held responsible as a fiduciary. Courts look to whether the employer was acting in a business capacity or as plan administrator on a case-by-case basis. An employer is not acting in a fiduciary capacity when the tasks are purely ministerial, such as processing claims, applying plan eligibility rules, and communicating with employees.[46] The decision to amend pension plans resulting in depriving employees of unreduced early retirement benefits was a business decision even though it was made by corporate officers who were also the plan's trustees. However, if, as plan trustees, the officers had cooperated in creating a surplus and diverting it so that it would not be reached by the employees, they would have been acting in a fiduciary capacity.[47] Similarly, where the termination of plan benefits was not motivated by a desire to save money or to destroy employee benefits, no fiduciary duty was found.[48] When severance benefits are contingent and unaccrued, an employer may unilaterally amend or eliminate the benefits plan without violating ERISA.[49] An employer is free to alter or eliminate severance benefits (which are usually solely funded by the employer) without consideration of the employees' interests. An employer does not owe its employees a fiduciary duty when it amends or abolishes a severance benefit plan.[50]

Undertaking discretionary roles is the mark of a fiduciary, and a benefits administrator should be careful not to unwittingly step into a fiduciary role. In *Six Clinics Holding Corp. v. Cafcomp Systems, Inc.,*[51] a corporation that provided physical and occupational therapy services decided to institute a cafeteria plan for its employees. On the recommendation of its insurance agent, it chose to establish the service with Cafcomp, an employee benefits administration company that provided comprehensive cafeteria plan services, including plan design and plan administration. They entered into a contract that spelled out the agreement. About a year later, the health care corporation terminated the plan because it was worried about the legality of certain actions. It alleged that Cafcomp and its president were ERISA fiduciaries with respect to the plan and that they violated their fiduciary duties in at least four ways.

The court found that whether Cafcomp owed a fiduciary duty depended upon whether Cafcomp had discretionary authority with regard to the plan. Cafcomp contended that it was not a fiduciary, because it performed only ministerial functions relating to the plan, including processing claims, applying plan eligibility rules, preparing employee communications material, preparing government-required reports, orienting new participants, calculating benefits, and making recommendations to others for decisions with respect to plan administration. It argued that the employer company maintained complete and final authority with regard to all plan matters and also performed the nonfiduciary functions. However, the court held that the plan administrator was acting as fiduciary based on the written contract. Specifically, the agreement listed numerous services that Cafcomp agreed to provide, including legal documentation, including any updates and amendments "as Cafcomp deems necessary"; preparation of annual reports "as required in the judgment of Cafcomp"; and transmittals of SPDs "as required in the judgment of Cafcomp." While some of these activities involve nonfiduciary functions, such as the preparation of government-required documents, Cafcomp appeared to have discretionary authority with regard to these functions. The agreement also provided that Cafcomp had the authority to amend the plan. Furthermore, Cafcomp's promotional material indicated that it assumed the role of a fiduciary by stating that it would assume the cost of maintaining the plan and would amend it as needed to ensure compliance with the law. The legal work would be provided by Cafcomp's law firm. There is no indication that Cafcomp would have to obtain approval for any changes to the plan.

Design/Administration Distinction

The design/administration distinction is used to determine if fiduciary duties attach. An employer's inclusion of a penalty provision in a benefits plan was found to be a management decision.[52] A decision to terminate pension plans, depriving the employees of unreduced early retirement benefits, was held to be a business decision and not made in a fiduciary capacity. If, as plan trustees, the corporate officers had cooperated in creating surplus and diverting it in order to prevent the funds from being reached by the employees, a breach of fiduciary duty would have been found.[53]

An employer registered his girlfriend as a full-time employee, and the insurance company enrolled her in the benefits plan. The employer confirmed her status as a full-time employee by remitting monthly premiums. She was later diagnosed with lung cancer, was hospitalized, and died. Her medical services were paid for by the insurance company, which later sued the employer for improper administration. The court found that the employer was not acting in a fiduciary capacity and could not be sued under ERISA (but could be liable for restitution under a common law theory). The employer was not acting in a discretionary capacity but merely performing ministerial functions. The determination of eligibility for participation or benefits, the maintenance of service and employment records, the calculation of benefits, and claims processing are merely ministerial and not fiduciary duties.[54]

Ensuring the administration of financially sound plans is critical to ERISA.[55] In *Varity v. Howe*,[56] the Supreme Court considered the question of whether an employer who was also the plan administrator was acting in a fiduciary or employer capacity when it persuaded employees to switch employers. The employees were participants in, and beneficiaries of, Massey-Ferguson's self-funded employee welfare benefit plan—an ERISA-protected plan that Massey-Ferguson itself administered. They claimed that the administrator, through trickery, led them to withdraw from the plan and to forfeit their benefits. They sought to be reinstated as participants in the employer's ERISA plan. The lower courts entered judgment in the employees' favor, and the Supreme Court reviewed that decision. Among the issues considered was whether the employer acted in its capacity as an ERISA "fiduciary" when it significantly and deliberately misled the beneficiaries. The employees used to work for Massey-Ferguson, Inc., a farm equipment manufacturer, and a wholly owned subsidiary of the petitioner, Varity Corporation. In the mid-1980s, Varity became concerned that some of Massey-Ferguson's divisions were losing too much money and developed a business plan and reorganization plan to deal with the problem.

Among the obligations that Varity hoped the reorganization would eliminate were those arising from the Massey-Ferguson benefit plan's promises to pay medical and other nonpension benefits to employees of Massey-Ferguson's money-losing divisions. Rather than terminate those benefits directly (as it had retained the right to do), Varity attempted to avoid the undesirable fallout that could have accompanied cancellation by inducing the failing divisions' employees to switch employers and thereby voluntarily release Massey-Ferguson from its obligation to provide them benefits (effectively substituting the new, self-funded Massey Combines benefit plan for the former Massey-Ferguson plan).

To persuade the employees of the failing divisions to accept the change of employer and benefit plan, Varity called them together at a special meeting and talked to them about Massey

Combines' future business outlook, its likely financial viability, and the security of their employee benefits. The thrust of Varity's remarks was that the employees' benefits would remain secure if they voluntarily transferred to Massey Combines. In the spring of 1986, Varity summoned the employees of Massey-Ferguson's money-losing divisions to a meeting at Massey-Ferguson's corporate headquarters for a 30-minute presentation. The employees saw a 90-second videotaped message from Ivan Porter, a Varity vice president and Massey Combines' newly appointed president. They also received four documents: (1) a several-page, detailed comparison between the employee benefits offered by Massey-Ferguson and those offered by Massey Combines; (2) a question-and-answer sheet; (3) a transcript of the Porter videotape; and (4) a cover letter with an acceptance form. Each of these documents discussed employee benefits and benefit plans, some briefly in general terms and others at length and in detail. After the presentation, about 1,500 Massey-Ferguson employees accepted Varity's assurances and voluntarily agreed to the transfer. Massey Combines ended its first year with a loss of $88 million and ended its second year in a receivership, under which its employees lost their nonpension benefits. Varity argued that when it communicated with its Massey-Ferguson workers about transferring to Massey Combines, it was not administering or managing the plan; rather, it was acting only in its capacity as an employer and not as a plan administrator.

The District Court, however, held that when the misrepresentations regarding employee benefits were made, Varity was wearing its "fiduciary," as well as its "employer," hat. The court determined that the key meeting was about benefits, for the documents described them in detail, explained the similarity between past and future plans in principle, and assured the employees that they would continue to receive similar benefits in practice. The court concluded that the basic message conveyed to the employees was that transferring from Massey-Ferguson to Massey Combines would not significantly undermine the security of their benefits. The Supreme Court concluded that Varity spoke, in significant part, in its capacity as plan administrator and that it had breached its fiduciary duties by deliberately misrepresenting the financial strength of the company.

PENSIONS

"'Employee pension benefit plan' or 'pension plan' means 'any plan, fund or program' that provides retirement income or results in deferral of income until the termination of employment."[57] These pension plans are regulated by ERISA.[58] Retirement plans provide incentives to the employees to remain with the organization, and they are an easy way to build up savings for retirement.

Qualified Retirement Plans

There are many types of retirement plans. Qualified retirement plans are attractive because both the participant and the employer benefit from their preferential tax treatment. The participant is not taxed until benefits are distributed, and the employer's contributions are deductible when made.[59] The Small Business Job Protection Act of 1996 simplifies pension requirements for small businesses. It repeals Salary Reduction Simplified Employee Pensions (SARSEPs) but grandfathers in SARSEPs created before January 1, 1997. The Act creates the Savings Incentive Match Plan for Employees (SIMPLE). SIMPLE plans are designed to simplify the procedures and requirements in which employers can offer pension plans. The benefits of SIMPLE are that it eliminates discrimination testing, top-heavy determinations, and some funding requirements that are found in other pension plans. To qualify for SIMPLE plans, an employer must have 100 or fewer employees and must not offer another retirement plan. Under SIMPLE, employees can contribute up to $6,000 to the retirement plan. The employer either matches the employee's contribution (the match cannot exceed 3 percent of the employee's compensation) or contributes up to 2 percent of compensation for each eligible employee. All contributions must be fully vested. Distributions from a SIMPLE plan are included in income. An early withdrawal penalty tax is assessed.[60]

Both defined contribution plans and defined benefit plans are qualified retirement plans. A qualified retirement plan must be a definite written program, be communicated to the employees, be permanent, and prohibit the use or diversion of funds for purposes other than the exclusive benefit of employees or their beneficiaries.[61] Examples of qualified retirement plans are money purchase pension plans, target benefit plans, profit-sharing plans;[62] thrift or savings plans; 401(k) plans; stock bonus plans; employee stock ownership plans; SEPs; savings incentive match plans for employees are included in defined contribution plans. Plans that are not defined contribution plans are termed *defined benefit plans*. Retirement benefits are easily determined in a defined benefit plan.

Vesting

Benefits are vested in a qualified retirement plan.[63] This means that the participant has a nonforfeitable right to the accrued benefits in the defined benefit plan. The federal law provides two minimum vesting schedules.[64] Either one may be used by the employer.

The Five Year Vesting Schedule provides that the employee is not vested until after five years of service. For example, Nurse Sue participates in a defined benefit plan at the Able HMO, which follows a five-year vesting schedule. She has an opportunity to move to a better paying position at the Better HMO. However, since she has been employed at Able for four years, she is not yet vested in the plan. She decided not to take the new position because her accrued benefits outweigh the higher salary offered.

A Seven Year Vesting Schedule is also permissible. Until working for three years, an employee is not vested at all. After three years of employment, the employee is 20 percent vested; after four years, 40 percent vested; after five years, 60 percent vested; after six years, 80 percent vested; and after seven years or more, 100 percent vested.[65] Using the example above, if Nurse Sue left Able, she would be entitled to 40 percent of her accrued benefits.

This rule works for single employer and multiemployer plans. Prior to 1997, multiemployer plans were subject to special vesting schedules. The differences were eliminated in the Small Business Job Protection Act of 1996 (SBJPA '96), effective for plan years beginning on or after the earlier of (1) the later date of either January 1, 1997, or the date on which the last of the collective bargaining agreements pursuant to which the plan is maintained terminates or (2) January 1, 1999, for participants with an hour of service after the effective date.

Funding and Eligibility

Qualified retirement plans must be funded by annual contributions by the organization, and the employer must intend to support the plan for a number of years.[66] A qualified retirement fund does not have to be offered to all categories of employees. Generally, exclusions are based on age and length of service. Nondiscrimination rules apply. Exclusions must be specified in the qualified retirement plan. Other exclusions are permissible under the law.[67] Prior to the enactment of the Small Business Job Protection Act of '96, there were minimum participation requirements.[68] These are now repealed. Effective after December 31, 1996, defined benefit plans must benefit no fewer than the lesser of 50 employees or the greater of either 40 percent of all employees or two employees.[69]

Reporting Requirements for Qualified Plans

If a defined contribution plan is offered, then the plan administrator has the duty to comply with numerous regulations, keep records for employee and employer contribution savings plans, reconcile the assets, and coordinate with trust accountants. If a defined benefits plan is offered, then the plan must comply with the regulations and government reporting rules, and the plan administrator will also work on plan design and nonqualified plan accounting.

The benefits administrator should know the filing requirements for qualified pension plans. Civil penalties may be assessed against the employer or plan administrator for late and/or incomplete filings, and extensions are available. Criminal sanctions may be applied for willful violation, false statements, and concealment of or failure to disclose any fact necessary to complete the reports. The responsibility to file the reports timely is on the employer or on the plan administrator, and it is not a defense that a third party was supposed to file the report.[70]

The 5500 series of reports are filed for most pension and welfare benefit plans that are subject to ERISA. An employer is required to file an annual report for each qualified retirement plan for each plan year that the plan has assets. The number of plan participants in the qualified retirement pension plan determines exactly which form is filed. If any benefits are paid by an insurance company, then an Insurance Information Form is filed along with the annual report. The particular form that must be filed depends on the number of participants in the plan. Along with these forms, an Actuarial Information, Service Provider and Trustee Information, Employee Stock Ownership form, Financial Schedules, Annual Return of Fiduciary of Employee Benefit Trust, and Annual Registration Statement Identifying Separated Participants with Deferred Vested Benefits are also attached as applicable. If the plan is a calendar year plan, then the forms are due by July 31. If it is not a calendar year plan, then they are due on the last date of the seventh month following the close of the plan year. The rule is different for a Short Plan Year (a plan year that is shorter than 12 months). Additional forms are filed with the Department of Labor (DOL) and the PBGC. The 1995 Delinquent Filer Voluntary Compliance Program[71] reduces penalties for late filing of annual reports.

Nonqualified Plans

A small health care employer may choose to offer a nonqualified plan. While the employer does not get a current deduction for contributions made to the plan, it does not have to fund the plan, either. The participant is not taxed until benefits are distributed in a nonqualified, unfunded plan.[72] An unfunded, nonqualified plan has no reporting or bookkeeping requirements.[73]

Effect of Merger on Pensions

If the health care organization mergers, either the pension plan will be terminated at the time of the merger and the payout will occur at the time of retirement, or a lump-sum distribution will be made that can be rolled over into another retirement plan. The retirement plan can be kept active and remain separate or can be merged with the acquiring company's plan. Employee benefits administrators will need to inform the employees of their options and of the plans available under the newly formed company. Even if written information cannot be made available immediately, information can be disseminated through meetings, through bulletin boards, and through the company's Internet web site. It is very important at the time of mergers and acquisitions that employees understand what will happen to their retirement plans and what their future options will be. Company morale and employee attitudes can depend on how employees perceive the new employer is treating them.

GROUP HEALTH PLANS INSURANCE

The four major types of group insurance coverage are life, accidental death and dismemberment, disability, and health or medical insurance.

Group Life Insurance

Life insurance provides cash payouts to beneficiaries if the participant dies while covered by the policy. It may be eligible for preferential tax treatment and can be offered as part of a cafeteria plan.

Group Accidental Death and Dismemberment

Accidental death and dismemberment insurance can be purchased as a rider to a life insurance policy. It provides coverage in the case of death or dismemberment within a certain period of time after an accident. In the case of death, the beneficiary receives a lump-sum benefit, and in the case of dismemberment, the participant receives the lump-sum benefit.

Group Disability Insurance

Group disability insurance covers loss of income due to a disability. The benefits are fixed at a percentage of the employee's salary. Short-term and long-term disability coverage is available. This benefit is important because it ensures employees against a loss of income at a critical time in their lives.

Health or Medical Insurance

Health insurance is critical to any employee benefit package. It can be provided in a variety of ways, and the benefit manager will be concerned with cost containment, services available, and the quality of care. Most states require that certain mandated benefits be included in a health care benefits contract offered by an insurer. Mandated benefits include coverage for alcohol treatment, substance abuse treatment, mental health services, preventive or diagnostic treatments, dependent children, and unpaid maternity and paternity leave for natural or adopted children.

Pharmacy Benefit Management

A prescription drug program is a benefit offered as a supplement to a health benefits plan. It can be either part of a major medical plan or a free-standing plan. It is often a fringe benefit negotiated by a collective bargaining agreement. Participants fill their prescriptions at a network pharmacy or by mail. Participants pay a monthly fee, and a copayment is paid when drugs are actually purchased. Drugs bought at nonparticipating pharmacies require payment by the employee who then files a reimbursement claim for the reasonable and customary cost less the deductible.[74] Since HMOs often offer prescription drug plans to their patients, it may be particularly economical for an HMO or other health care organization to offer this benefit to its employees. Restricted pharmacy network agreements contain particulars on matters of billing, reimbursement, eligibility, protection of information, quality assurance, and auditing.[75] The benefits administrator should request utilization review reports and integrated claims information processing from the pharmacy benefit manager program. These reports provide information on utilization, claims, and cost analysis.

Long-Term Care

Long-term care is a welfare benefit that is becoming more popular and prevalent. While providing long-term care presents challenges, health care associations may have an edge in its provision. Long-term care insurance is important to employees because many employees are responsible for aging and/or disabled parents and spouses. Nursing home and home health care is expensive, and employees realize that government-sponsored programs will not cover the enormous costs of long-term care.

Managing a long-term care benefits program may be difficult. First, there is a general shortage of quality long-term health care. Second, long-term care benefits need to coordinate with other available medical coverage and government funds. Third, it may be difficult to determine adequate levels of coverage and whether the benefits should be based on maximum daily benefits or lifetime maximum benefits. The health care benefits administrator may want to survey the employees and find out what their ideal long-term benefits would cover and how the program would be designed. Further, the health care benefits specialist should also know that since long-term care is not a statutory benefit, it cannot be included in a cafeteria plan.

Financing Group Health Plans

If a single health care organization is too small to offer these expected and necessary benefits to its employees, then it can often become part of a multiple employer trust (MET), which will offer a high level of benefits at a cost otherwise available only to large employers. In a MET, the policy is issued to a trust, and the master contract is issued to a trustee. Another way for a small health care organization to offer group coverage is through a labor union. In this case, the policy is issued to a trust managed by both the union and employer representatives. An insurance professional consultant, broker, or agent can help the health care organization decide which benefits packages to purchase and through which insurance company.

ERISA Requirements

Group health plans are subject to ERISA requirements since they are a "welfare benefit." Administrators of group health plans may transmit SPDs and SMMs through electronic media on or after June 1, 1997. HIPAA's interim disclosure rules provide a "safe harbor" for using e-mail to furnish group health plan SPDs, summaries of "material reductions in covered services or benefits," and other SMMs. Employees must effectively be able to access at their worksite documents furnished in electronic form. Participants also continue to have a right to receive the disclosures in paper form on request and free of charge.[76]

State Laws

Group health insurance policies are regulated by states and direct a minimum level of benefits that must be offered. Some states exempt "small employers" from the statutory requirements. Small employers also have restricted premium rates that can be charged by insurance companies. Most states require that basic coverage be offered in group plans for small employers. When a state passes a law that requires all employee benefit plans to pay pregnancy-related benefits to employees, then a benefit provider must alter the plan to comply with a specific state law.[77] Similarly, when a state mandates that an employee benefit plan provide minimum mental health coverage, then a plan administrator must modify the plan or violate state law.[78] Many states require that all group policies offer alcohol and drug abuse treatment coverage. Mental health coverage is also required by most states. A few states leave these as options for the employer to decide. It should be noted that even where the option is up to the employer, minimum yearly inpatient, outpatient, and lifetime coverages are required if the benefits are offered.

Maternity and dependent coverage are similarly required to be part of all group health insurance contracts in many states. Other states leave the coverage option up to the employer participating in a group health insurance contract. Every state requires that newborns and adopted infants are covered. Fertility treatments, by and large, are not mandated in most states, although some specify the type and number of fertility treatments that must be covered. Mandated coverage for preventive care for children varies from state to state. Some mandate coverage to age 18; others to age 16; others to ages 2, 5, and 6. Some states require that immunizations are covered, and others include mandatory lead screening coverage.

Most states do not mandate coverage for particular illnesses, such as Alzheimer's disease, diabetes, or acquired immunodeficiency syndrome (AIDS). However, many states mandate coverage for joint-related disorders, and only a few states leave it as an employer option. Mammograms are mandated by most states, while mastectomies and reconstructive surgery are not. Home health care is included in mandatory coverage; hospice care tends to be left to the option of the employer. Almost every state requires that coverage for visits to an optometrist is offered, but coverage for dentists and podiatrists is not consistently required.

While self-funded employers can change the terms of the medical coverage offered by placing caps or exclusions on covering particular conditions or treatments,[79] health care organizations should be aware of the numerous federal regulations.

FEDERAL AND STATE REGULATION

Health care benefits are subject to numerous federal laws and regulations. These include the Pregnancy Discrimination Act (PDA), the Newborns' and Mothers' Health Protection Act of 1996 (NMHPA), the Family Medical Leave Act (FMLA), the Age Discrimination in Employment Act (ADEA), the Mental Health Parity Act (MHPA) of 1996, the Americans with Disabilities Act

(ADA), and the Omnibus Budget Reconciliation Act (OBRA) '93. State law also has an impact on health care coverage, and the health care employer needs to understand the relationship between the federal and state laws. The insurer is usually responsible for being sure that the benefits plans offered comply with the law.

PDA

The PDA applies to all private employers with 15 or more employees for each working day for 20 or more weeks in the current or preceding year. It basically mandates that pregnancy and childbirth be treated the same way that other disabilities or medical conditions are treated under the health care coverage offered.

NMHPA

The NMHPA is federal legislation effective January 1998 requiring health plans that provide coverage for the hospital stay of new mothers to allow them to remain at least 48 hours after a "normal" delivery and 96 hours for Caesarean delivery.[80] Penalties cannot be imposed, and incentives cannot be given for either staying in the hospital or for leaving early. NMHPA does not prevent a group health plan, insurance company, or HMO from imposing deductibles, coinsurance, or other cost-sharing measures for health benefits relating to hospital stays in connection with childbirth as long as such cost-sharing measures are not greater than those imposed on any preceding portion of the hospital stay.

FMLA

The FMLA is federal legislation affecting employers with 50 or more employees. It mandates up to 12 weeks of unpaid leave time for employees to care for a newborn or adopted child within 12 months of the birth or adoption. It also covers up to 12 weeks unpaid leave for a serious illness or the serious illness of a spouse, child, or parent. The employee must return to the same or equivalent position held before the leave. Eligibility requirements and other details are covered later in this book.

The federal FMLA provides the minimum rights that states must provide. These can be extended by the states. Some states have increased the number of benefits required under the FMLA. While, for many states, these modifications are only imposed on state employers (i.e., Arkansas, Colorado, Delaware, Florida, and Texas, to name a few), in other states, any employer with a minimum number of employees must grant leave under its FMLA regulations. Most states require a birth/adoption or illness for leave to be granted, but some also find that attendance at a school conference is an acceptable reason for leave. Lengthy leaves can affect other benefits, and most states require the employee to pay the premiums for continued health and group life insurance.

ADEA

The ADEA prohibits discrimination in employment against employees who are aged 40 and older. The same health coverage offered by employers with 20 or more employees to younger employees must be offered to all active employees and their spouses despite age or Medicare eligibility. Cost-justified reductions are permitted for life and disability insurance.

MHPA

The MHPA was signed into law on September 26, 1996. This law provides for parity in the application of limits to certain mental health benefits. Under the MHPA, group health plans, insurance companies, and HMOs offering mental health benefits will not be allowed to set annual or lifetime limits on mental health benefits that are lower than any such limits for medical and surgical benefits. A plan that does not impose an annual or lifetime limit on medical and surgical benefits may not impose such a limit on mental health benefits. The MHPA's provisions, however, do not apply to benefits for substance abuse or chemical dependency.

Health plans are not required to include mental health coverage in their benefits package. The requirements under the MHPA apply only to plans offering mental health benefits. Plans may continue to set the terms and conditions (such as cost-sharing and limits on the number of visits or days of coverage) for the amount, duration, and scope of mental health benefits. There are two significant exceptions to these new rules. The mental health parity requirements do not apply to small employers who have between 2 and 50 employees or to any group health plan whose costs increase 1 percent or more due to the application of these requirements.

The MHPA requirements apply to group health plans for plan years beginning on or after January 1, 1998. A so-called "sunset" provision provides that these requirements will cease to apply to benefits for services furnished on or after September 30, 2001. The MHPA does not have a separate effective date for collectively bargained plans.

ADA

The ADA is federal legislation affecting employers with 15 or more employees. It prohibits discrimination against disabled persons in hiring, firing, pay, promotion, training, and so forth. An employer showing that accommodating the disabled person would cause an "undue hardship" is exempt from making ADA-legislated changes. In the hiring process, an employer cannot take into account the extra expense a disabled employee would have on the health care benefits.

OBRA '93

Qualified medical child support orders (QMCSOs) are court orders or judgments that mandate a child's right to receive health benefits. OBRA '93 requires group health plans to administer these benefits.[81] The plan administrator has the duty to notify the parties of the procedures used to determine whether the court order is "qualified" and to give notice of the decision to the parties.

HIPAA

HIPAA places requirements on employer-sponsored group health plans, insurance companies, and HMOs and affects the preexisting conditions exclusion offered by group health plans. HIPAA includes changes that accomplish the following:

- Limit exclusions for preexisting conditions.
- Prohibit discrimination against employees and dependents based on their health status.
- Guarantee renewability and availability of health coverage to certain employers and individuals.
- Protect many workers who lose health coverage by providing better access to individual health insurance coverage.

HIPAA provides that all small employers (2 to 50 employees) and employees applying during the time they first become eligible must be accepted for insurance coverage. However, certain types of coverage are excluded from HIPAA.[82]

Under HIPAA, a group health plan or a health insurance issuer offering group health insurance coverage may impose a preexisting condition exclusion with respect to a participant or beneficiary only if the following apply:

1. A preexisting condition exclusion must relate to a condition for which medical advice, diagnosis, care, or treatment was recommended or received during the 6-month period prior to an individual's enrollment date.
2. A preexisting condition exclusion may not last for more than 12 months (18 months for late enrollees) after an individual's enrollment date.
3. This 12- (or 18-) month period must be reduced by the number of days of the individual's prior creditable coverage, excluding coverage before any break in coverage of 63 days or more.

Crediting Time

A new employer's plan is required to credit the length of time that the employee had continuous health coverage. This reduces the 12-month exclusion period due to preexisting medical conditions that is present in most health benefits plans. A new employee who already had 12 months of continuous health coverage (without a break in coverage of 63 days or more), will not have to start over with a new 12-month exclusion for any preexisting conditions.

Waiting Period

A plan must reduce an individual's preexisting condition exclusion period by the number of days of an individual's creditable coverage. However, a plan is not required to take into account any days of creditable coverage that precede a break in coverage of 63 days or more ("significant break in coverage"). A plan generally receives information about an individual's creditable coverage from a certificate furnished by a prior plan or issuer (e.g., an insurance company or HMO).

Affiliation periods run concurrently with any waiting period under a plan, may not last for more than 2 months (3 months for late enrollees), and are only allowed for HMOs that do not impose preexisting condition exclusion periods. If the employee or dependent is a late enrollee or a special enrollee, any period before enrollment is not a waiting period.

Preexisting Conditions

Preexisting condition exclusions cannot be applied to pregnancy, regardless of whether the woman had previous coverage. In addition, a preexisting condition exclusion cannot be applied to a newborn, adopted child under age 18, or a child under 18 placed for adoption as long as the child became covered under the health plan within 30 days of birth, adoption, or placement for adoption and provided the child does not incur a subsequent 63-day or longer break in coverage.

Many health plans do not exclude coverage for preexisting conditions. A plan must state if it has a preexisting condition exclusion period (and can only exclude coverage for a preexisting condition after notification). Notification must also state the right to show that prior creditable coverage is available to reduce the preexisting condition exclusion period.

If the plan does apply a preexisting condition exclusion period, the plan must make a determination regarding creditable coverage and the length of any preexisting condition exclusion period. The determination must be made within a reasonable time after presentation of the certificate. The plan must notify the participant of this determination if, after considering all evidence of creditable coverage, the plan will still impose a preexisting condition exclusion period. The notice must also state the basis of the determination, including the source and substance of any information on which the plan relied and the appeals procedure. The plan may modify its initial determination if it later determines that the participant does not have the claimed creditable coverage. The plan must notify the participant of its reconsideration. Until a final determination is made, the plan must act in accordance with its initial determination for purposes of approving medical services.

The maximum length of a preexisting condition exclusion period is 12 months after the enrollment date (18 months in the case of a "late enrollee"). A late enrollee is an individual who enrolls in a plan other than on either the earliest date on which coverage can become effective under the terms of the plan or on a special enrollment date.

Certificate of Creditable Coverage

A certificate of creditable coverage must be provided automatically to the participant by the plan or issuer (1) when the participant loses coverage under the plan, (2) when the participant becomes entitled to elect COBRA continuation coverage, and (3) when COBRA continuation coverage ceases as well as upon request from the previous plan or insurance company within 24 months of the end of coverage.

If a new employee does not have a certificate of coverage, proof of creditable coverage (as well as any waiting periods) may be shown by documentation or other evidence, such as pay stubs, that reflect a deduction for health insurance, explanation of benefits forms (EOBs), or verification by a physician or former health care benefits provider. To avoid duplication of certificates, a plan may contract with the issuer to provide the certificate. Furthermore, if any entity (including a third-party administrator) provides a certificate to an individual, no other party is required to provide the certificate. Even plans that do not impose a preexisting condition exclusion period (and the issuers that provide coverage under these plans) have to provide certificates. Health benefits personnel should be aware that if the employee, a former plan, and the new plan for which application is being made agree, the information may be transferred by telephone. The participant still has a right to a written certificate.

A plan or issuer must make reasonable efforts to collect the necessary information for dependents and include it on the certificate. However, an automatic certificate for a dependent is not required to be issued until the plan or issuer knows (or, making reasonable efforts, should know) of the dependent's loss of coverage. This information can be collected annually, such as during an open enrollment period.

A certificate that is issued automatically should reflect the most recent period of continuous coverage. A certificate that is issued upon request should reflect each period of continuous coverage ending within 24 months prior to the date of request. Neither certificate is required to reflect more than 18 months of creditable coverage that is not interrupted by a break in coverage of 63 days or more. Group health plans and issuers are not required to provide certificates before June 1, 1997. Generally, the certification requirements apply to periods of coverage that occur after June 30, 1996, and certificates must be provided when coverage ceases under the plan. Through June 30, 1998, a plan or issuer may satisfy its obligation to provide a written certificate regarding the coverage of a dependent by providing the name of the participant covered by the plan and specifying the type of coverage provided (such as family coverage or employee-plus-spouse coverage). However, if requested to provide a certificate relating to a dependent, the plan must make reasonable efforts to obtain and provide the name of the dependent.

Health care benefits personnel should also be aware that current employees who were denied coverage based on a preexisting condition must be credited with coverage accumulated prior to the enrollment date. Creditable coverage does not include coverage consisting solely of "excepted benefits," such as coverage solely for dental or vision benefits.

Alternative Method

A plan or issuer may elect the "alternative method" for crediting coverage for all employees. Under the alternative method of counting creditable coverage, the plan or issuer determines the amount of an individual's creditable coverage for any of the five specified categories of benefits: (1) mental health, (2) substance abuse treatment, (3) prescription drugs, (4) dental care, and (5) vision care. The standard method (described above) is used to determine an individual's creditable coverage for benefits that are not within any of the five categories that a plan or issuer may use. (The plan or issuer may use some or all of these categories.) When using the alternative method, the plan or issuer looks to see if an individual has coverage within a category of benefits (regardless of the specific level of benefits provided within that category). The health care benefits administrator should be aware that a former employee is entitled to information about coverage under the five categories of benefits.

Health-Based Exclusion

Individuals may not be excluded from coverage under the terms of the plan, or charged more for benefits offered by a plan or issuer, based on specified factors related to health status. Group health plans and issuers may not establish rules for eligibility (including continued eligibility) of any individual to enroll under the terms of the plan based on "health-status–related factors." These factors are health status, medical condition (physical or mental), claims experience, receipt of health care, medical history, genetic information, evidence of insurability, or disability. However, plans may establish limits or restrictions on benefits or coverage for similarly situated individuals. In addition, plans may change covered services or benefits if they give participants notice of such "material reductions" within 60 days after the change is adopted. Also, plans may not require an individual to pay a premium or contribution greater than that for a similarly situated individual based on a health-status–related factor.

Special Enrollment

Group health plans and health insurance issuers are required to permit certain employees and dependents special enrollment rights. These rights are provided both to employees who were eligible but declined enrollment in the plan when first offered because they were covered under another plan and to individuals upon the marriage, birth, adoption, or placement for adoption of a new dependent. These special enrollment rights permit these individuals to enroll without having to wait until the plan's next regular enrollment period. A special enrollee is not treated as a late enrollee. Therefore, the maximum preexisting condition exclusion period that may be applied to a special enrollee is 12 months, and the 12 months are reduced by the special enrollee's creditable coverage. (A newborn, adopted child, or child placed for adoption cannot be subject to a preexisting condition exclusion period if the child is enrolled within 30 days of birth, adoption, or placement for adoption.) A plan must provide a description of the plan's special enrollment rights under HIPAA to anyone who declines coverage.

Renewal of Group Health Plans

It is the plan sponsor's option whether to have group health insurance coverage renewed. However, the issuer has the right to discontinue or refuse to renew group health insurance coverage if the employer, as plan sponsor, failed to pay premiums, committed fraud, violated participation or contribution rules, or if the issuer ceases to offer that particular coverage or moves outside the service area.

Disclosure

The interim disclosure rules permit the use of e-mail to furnish group health plan SPDs, summaries of "material reductions in covered services or benefits," and other SMMs and SPD changes. Employees must be able to effectively access at their worksite documents furnished in electronic form. Participants also continue to have a right to receive the disclosures in paper form on request and free of charge.[83]

Effective Dates

Group health plans must comply with all nondiscrimination, preexisting condition, and crediting of prior health coverage requirements at the beginning of the first plan year starting after June 30, 1997. If the group health plan is maintained pursuant to collective bargaining agreements that were ratified before August 21, 1996, the effective date of HIPAA is delayed. HIPAA's provisions apply to these plans on the later of either the first day of the plan year beginning on or after either the date on which the last collective bargaining agreement ends or July 1, 1997.

States' Options

States may impose stricter obligations on health insurance issuers in the seven areas listed below.[84] States may do the following:

- Shorten the 6-month "look-back" period prior to the enrollment date to determine what is a preexisting condition.
- Shorten the 12- and 18-month maximum preexisting condition exclusion periods.
- Increase the 63-day significant break in coverage period.
- Increase the 30-day period for newborns, adopted children, and children placed for adoption to enroll in the plan so that no preexisting condition exclusion period may be applied thereafter.

- Expand the prohibitions on conditions and people to whom a preexisting condition exclusion period may be applied beyond the "exceptions" described in federal law (the "exceptions" under federal law are for certain newborns, adopted children, children placed for adoption, and pregnancy).
- Require additional special enrollment periods.
- Reduce the maximum HMO affiliation period to less than 2 months (3 months for late enrollees).

Health care benefits administrators should check with their state insurance commissioner's office to find out their state's rules.

COBRA

COBRA 1985 provides employees and qualifying plan beneficiaries who lose coverage under an employer's group health plan with an option to continue in the group plan for a limited time at their own expense.[85] Congress enacted COBRA "to provide continued access to affordable private health insurance."[86] COBRA ensures that beneficiaries of an employer-sponsored health care plan will be able to maintain coverage even after the occurrence of specific statutorily enumerated events. The continuation coverage must be identical to that received by any similarly situated beneficiaries under the plan who have not experienced a "qualifying event."[87] Disability insurance is different from health insurance, and, therefore, there is no COBRA right to an extension of disability insurance,[88] nor does COBRA apply to life, accidental death, or dismemberment insurance.[89] Three types of employers are not subject to COBRA requirements: (1) any governmental plan,[90] (2) any church plan,[91] and (3) an employer employing fewer than 20 employees on a typical business day within the calendar year.[92]

Maintenance of Group Health Plan

An employer is subject to COBRA requirements if it maintains a group health plan for the benefit of its employees by either direct or indirect contributions to the plan.[93] Indirect contribution to a plan is made where the employer makes a plan available to the employees but does not pay for any part of the premiums. The test to determine whether an employer maintains a health care benefit plan subject to COBRA requirements is easy to use. A plan is maintained by the employer if the benefits would cost more to the plan participants if the coverage were not offered by the employer. If an employer maintains more than one plan, continuation coverage must be provided even when the particular plan under which the employee was covered is terminated.[94]

Small Employer Exemption

A small employer offering a group health plan is not required to offer COBRA coverage to a qualified beneficiary if the qualifying event occurs during a year following a calendar year in which the employer normally employed fewer than 20 employees on a typical business day.[95] For example, COBRA benefits were properly denied to a quadriplegic employee injured in a nonwork-related accident where only 12 employees had been working for the employer in the calendar year before the year in which coverage was terminated.[96] For purposes of applying the small group exception to COBRA requirements, the employees and officers who are common to all members of a common entity are considered to be a single employee.[97]

To calculate whether a small business exemption existed, one company used its computerized payroll check register covering each weekly pay period. The company combined the number of full-time, part-time, contract, and temporary employees for each pay period. It then assumed that all persons employed in a given week worked each day of the pay period. From these figures, the company calculated the number of work days during the year in which it employed fewer than 20 persons and the number in which it employed greater than 20 persons.[98] An employer subject to COBRA during one year must offer COBRA rights to persons who became qualified beneficiaries during that year even if the size of the company is currently reduced to fewer than 20 employees.

For example, Able Health Care has 30 employees in Year 1 and offers group health coverage to them. It therefore is subject to COBRA. In Year 2, Able Health Care only has 20 employees but still must offer COBRA rights due to its size in Year 1. In Year 3, however, Able only has to offer COBRA to the covered employees and beneficiaries who became qualified beneficiaries during Year 2.

Qualifying Events

COBRA coverage is triggered by "qualifying events":

- the death of the covered employee
- termination except if due to the employee's "gross misconduct"
- reduction in hours of the covered employee
- divorce or legal separation of the covered employee
- the eligibility of the covered employee to receive Medicare benefits[99]
- a previously dependent child who is no longer dependent
- the employer's bankruptcy[100]

Termination occurs when an employee actually stops working for an employer, not when he or she gives notice of intention to do so. Sometimes this happens simultaneously. Other times, an employee may give notice days, weeks, or even months in advance of actual termination. In the interim, the employment relationship continues. Only when the employee ultimately leaves the company or has his or her hours reduced to the point of losing coverage, does a qualifying event occur, thereby triggering the administrator's duties under COBRA.[101] Failure to pay the premium on the health plan is not a qualifying event, and, therefore, COBRA rights are not triggered for loss of coverage.[102]

Gross misconduct is not defined by the statute, and the definition remains murky. While it has been held to include misappropriation of funds; permitting the employee to resign caused the termination to be voluntary rather than for gross misconduct, and COBRA rights were triggered;[103] dismissal for a single incident of spreading confidential information about the employer was found to be termination for poor judgment rather than for gross misconduct.[104] Courts have looked to the state law's definition of *gross misconduct* in statutes dealing with ineligibility for unemployment due to termination for gross misconduct.[105] However, it has also been held that the definition must be interpreted under federal and not state law.[106] Note that if a multiemployer plan document gives the plan administrator the authority to decide if an employee has been terminated for reasons other than gross misconduct or has had a reduction of hours,[107] notice from the employer to the plan administration is not necessary.[108]

Prior to enactment of HIPAA, a qualified beneficiary was entitled to the 11-month disability extension only if he or she was disabled at the time that the covered employee suffered the termination or reduction in hours of employment. COBRA benefits are now extended for an additional 11 months if a qualified beneficiary is disabled during the first 60 days of COBRA continuation coverage.[109] This extends COBRA coverage for up to 29 months from the date of the qualifying event. This extension of coverage is also available to nondisabled family members who are entitled to COBRA continuation coverage.[110]

The definition of *qualified beneficiary* is extended where group health coverage is lost due to the employer's filing for bankruptcy under U.S.C. Title 11. It includes covered employees who retired within one year before or after the date of the bankruptcy if the loss of coverage includes a "substantial elimination" of coverage.[111]

Notice

Notice of COBRA benefits is given twice, once when coverage begins and then again when COBRA rights are triggered by a qualifying event. The duty to give notice falls on the parties to the plan. These parties are the employer, the trustee, and the insurer. Penalties may be assessed for failure to give notice.[112] Failure to advise a beneficiary when the first premium payment is due combined with other notice deficiencies renders notice invalid.[113]

Written notice of COBRA rights is given by the group health plan at the commencement of coverage. Both the employee and spouse are entitled to initial notice when coverage begins. Initial notice may be satisfied through the SPD given to all employees. However, this type of COBRA notice will not be sufficient if the SPD is not properly distributed.[114]

A second notice of COBRA rights is sent to the plan beneficiaries when a qualifying event occurs. The employee's knowledge of his or her COBRA rights does not relieve the parties of notification duties.[115] Both the employer and the plan administrator have duties regarding the second notice. First, the employer has a duty to give notice to the plan administrator of the occurrence of the following qualifying events:

- death of the covered employee[116]
- termination for reasons other than gross misconduct
- deduction of hours of employment
- employee's entitlement to Medicare benefits
- the employer's bankruptcy[117]

The employer must send notice within 30 days of the occurrence of the qualifying event. If this notice is not timely sent to the plan administrator, then the employer can be held liable.[118] The 30-day period applies even where the plan administrator and the employer are one and the same entity.[119] Although there is no specific language necessary for the notice to be sufficient, the court held that the word *cancel* marked next to the employee's name on the monthly premium statement did not serve as notice of a qualifying event to the plan administrator.

The plan administrator has a 14-day period from receipt of notice of the qualifying event to notify the COBRA beneficiaries of their right to continued coverage. The courts are divided on the issue of what constitutes sufficient notice to an employee's spouse upon termination,[120] but it is clear that a good faith effort to notify the spouse of COBRA rights must be made.[121]

The covered employee or a qualified beneficiary has a duty to report to the plan administrator the following qualifying events within 60 days of their occurrence:[122] divorce or legal separation of the covered employee and the cessation of dependency. Plan administrators must be sure to send notice of COBRA rights to the beneficiaries after receiving notice of the qualifying event. The duty to notify the plan administrator of a qualifying event does not arise if the qualified beneficiaries did not receive proper initial notice of their COBRA rights.[123] If the qualifying event is divorce, separation, or cessation of dependency, it is the beneficiary's and not the employee's health coverage that is in jeopardy. Where the plan administrator gave the COBRA notice to the covered employee to give to his ex-wife, notice was insufficient concerning the ex-wife. Notice requirements are satisfied by good faith compliance.[124] Adequate notification was found, however, because the insurer sent an identification card, premium statement, and benefits information to the ex-wife herself.[125] Summary judgment was found where the evidence showed that the employer sent a COBRA termination notice to the employee's correct address,[126] and proof that the notice was actually received is not required.[127]

Remedies for notice violations seek to put plaintiffs back in the same position they would have been in but for the COBRA violation.[128] The administrator bears the burden of proof that adequate COBRA notice was given since employers have a statutory record-keeping requirement.[129] Note that the term *plan administrator* refers to the entity charged with overall management of the health plan and not to the individual clerical administrators.[130] Damages are calculated by subtracting the deductibles or copayments as well as the premium the plaintiff would have paid if covered by COBRA from the medical bills incurred due to the lack of health care coverage.[131] Penalties and excise taxes may also be assessed against the employer and/or the plan administrator.[132] Defenses to the imposition of an excise tax include proof that (1) despite the use of reasonable diligence, the responsible parties neither knew nor would have known that a COBRA violation existed,[133] and (2) the failure was due to reasonable cause and not to willful neglect and that it was corrected within 30 days of the time the responsible parties knew or should have known of the failure.

Revision of COBRA Notice Requirements

COBRA notice requirements are confusing and are in the process of revision. The DOL is currently seeking to revise the COBRA notice requirements, and the benefits administrator should be on the lookout for new regulations. The DOL is looking into whether the notice should be required to include the following:

1. a description of the continuation coverage that the qualified beneficiary is entitled to elect
2. a description of the period over which such continuation coverage would be provided
3. a description of the premiums that the qualified beneficiary would be required to pay, including the manner in which such premiums were calculated, the dates on which payment would be due, the address to which payment should be sent, and the consequences of nonpayment
4. an explanation of the election process, including the period of time within which an election can be made, the consequences of electing or failing to elect continuation coverage, and the possibility of rescinding an election
5. an explanation of any rights that might arise to cause an extension of the maximum period of continuation coverage (such as with respect to any qualified beneficiary who is determined to be disabled within the first 60 days of continuation coverage) and the notice obligations imposed on any such qualified beneficiary.

The DOL is also considering whether to require that other information be included in the notice of right to elect continuation coverage, such as the significance of electing continuation coverage for rights granted by HIPAA or the FMLA and significant information relevant to the decision whether to elect continuation coverage. Another option is that inclusion of the information in the SPD, with a reference in the notice to the relevant information in the SPD, will be adequate notice.

The DOL is looking at the way in which notice requirements can be satisfied. E-mail messages are certain to be permissible means in the near future. Other areas of concern include the administrative procedures that plan administrators use to provide additional notices or information not expressly mandated in the COBRA provisions but that are necessary or useful. The DOL is looking at how the following areas are communicated to employees and beneficiaries: changes in the coverage provided under the group health plan (including changes in the issuer or service provider), open enrollment or election periods provided under the plan, enforcement due dates for continuation coverage premiums, and implementation of the termination of continuation coverage and available conversion options.

Election of COBRA Benefits

The qualified beneficiary must notify the plan administrator that he or she wants to continue health coverage during the election period. The election period begins on or before the date on which coverage terminates due to the qualifying event. It ends at least 60 days after the later of either the date on which coverage would end or the date on which notice is sent to the qualified beneficiary.[134] The election period may be extended by the plan.[135] COBRA coverage is retroactive from the date it would otherwise have ended. The election period is tolled in certain situations. These include where the SPD did not specify a 60-day election period and where the qualified beneficiary cannot make a COBRA election due to physical or mental disability.[136] The appointment of a personal representative ends the tolling period.[137]

An election of continuation coverage by a qualified beneficiary is deemed to include an election of all the beneficiaries who would lose coverage by the same qualifying event. However, a beneficiary cannot decline coverage on behalf of another beneficiary.[138]

Continuation Coverage

The COBRA coverage must be the same as the coverage provided to similar beneficiaries to whom a qualifying event did not occur. The qualified beneficiaries are entitled to participate in open enrollment period rights and to enroll new family members. A qualified beneficiary has the right to continue either all or part of the coverage received prior to the qualifying event. The issue is whether the benefits were offered under a single plan or multiple noncore plans. Generally, if a single plan provides core and noncore benefits, then the beneficiary can continue either all of the coverage or just the core coverage. If noncore benefits were offered under separate plans, such as a vision plan and a dental plan, then a qualified beneficiary can choose to continue any combination of the plans.[139]

Continuing coverage runs from the date of the qualifying event. Different maximum coverage periods apply depending on the nature of the qualifying event:

- *Termination or reduction of hours:* The continuing coverage is offered for 18 months after the occurrence of these qualifying events.
- *Second qualifying event (except bankruptcy) within the 18-month period:* The continuing coverage is extended for a maximum of 36 months from the date of the first qualifying event.[140]
- *Determination of disability under Title II or XVI of the Social Security Act at any time during the first 60 days of COBRA continuation coverage:* The 18th month coverage is extended to a maximum of 29 months. This 11-month disability extension applies to the nondisabled family members of a disabled qualified beneficiary who meets the requirements for the extension so long as those family members are also entitled to continuation coverage.[141]
- *Medicare eligibility:*[142] If an employee becomes entitled to Medicare, whether or not coverage is lost, and a second qualifying event occurs within 18 months of entitlement, then the period of continuation coverage for qualified beneficiaries is 36 months. The 36 months are counted from the date of Medicare entitlement.

Even before the maximum applicable coverage period expires, an employer may (but is not required to) terminate the COBRA coverage if any of the following occur:

- It no longer maintains any group health plan, including successor plans.[143]
- The qualified beneficiary does not pay the required premium.
- The qualified beneficiary becomes covered under a different group health plan.[144]

However, prior to terminating any COBRA coverage, a consultation with counsel is recommended. In the case of a multiemployer health insurance plan, the multiemployer plan remains responsible for COBRA-qualified employees where an employer withdraws from the multiemployer health insurance plan and establishes a new health plan for its remaining employees. The multiemployer plan sponsor is not relieved of its duty until the occurrence of an event listed in 29 U.S.C. § 1162(2). Nothing in the statute permits a plan sponsor of a multiemployer plan to terminate its COBRA obligation to qualified individuals because a participating employer subsequently sponsors its own plan for other covered persons.[145] Nonpayment of premiums is grounds for ending the COBRA benefits. The beneficiary has 45 days after first electing COBRA benefits to pay the premium.[146] Later payments must be made within a 30-day grace period after their due date or within a longer period if the plan permits.[147]

Significant Gap

Although the courts have been divided on whether coverage under a second plan terminates COBRA benefits,[148] the HIPAA amendments clarify that the mere fact of a preexisting insurance policy is not grounds for termination of COBRA rights. HIPAA changes became effective January 1, 1997, regardless of the date of any qualifying event. Among other changes, HIPAA amended the circumstances under which a group health plan may cease providing continuation coverage to a qualified beneficiary where that qualified beneficiary becomes covered under another group health plan. COBRA now provides that, if the new plan limits or excludes coverage for any preexisting condition of the qualified beneficiary, the plan providing continuation coverage cannot cease making continuation coverage available solely due to the fact that the beneficiary is participating in a second plan.

Fiduciary Liability

Fiduciary liability is determined under both ERISA and COBRA. For example, pursuant to ERISA, the plan administrator has personal liability for failure to send COBRA notices even when this duty is delegated.[149] Good faith, or lack of it, as well as prejudice to the beneficiary's rights will have a role in determining the size of the liability,[150] although courts have imposed penalties even where neither bad faith nor prejudice was shown.[151] COBRA rights are enforced by the IRS, the DOL, and the Department of Health and Human Services (HHS) as well as in a civil action brought by a qualified beneficiary.

Under ERISA, fiduciary status is determined by the function a person has and not by the person's actual status.[152] A fiduciary is subject to ERISA duties "to the extent" that he or she "exercises any authority or control respecting management or disposition of assets" or has any discretionary authority or discretionary responsibility in the administration of such plan.[153] Using this broad definition, fiduciary status was found where the individuals were not plan administrators but used plan assets to pay their company's creditors; were the only signatories on the company account; signed checks on that account, including checks payable to the plan, and decided which creditors were to be paid out of the company's general account and when those payments would be made.[154] An attorney rendering service to a plan is not a fiduciary so long as he does not exercise any authority over the plan other than the usual professional functions.[155] ERISA does not authorize legal damages against nonfiduciaries who participate in a fiduciary breach.[156] Breach of fiduciary duty was found for the employer's failure to advise a qualified beneficiary of the availability of COBRA benefits for her deceased husband's medical bills. The widow asked the employer whether a death benefit was available and did not ask about COBRA benefits for the medical bills. Nonetheless, since the inquiry was made during the COBRA election period, and the employer had sent notice of COBRA benefits, the failure to mention their availability was breach of fiduciary duty.[157]

McDowell v. Krawchison[158] is of particular interest to health care organizations. The defendant, Krawchison, owned and operated several chiropractic clinics in Ohio, Kentucky, and Indiana. He owned half the shares in three clinics and owned all the shares in the remainder. Most of the clinics were separately incorporated. The clinics provided health insurance to their employees through Medical Benefits Mutual Life Insurance Company. Krawchison obtained the insurance under a single plan for all the clinics. He hired McDowell, but, later that year, the clinic was bought, and the new owner terminated McDowell's employment. McDowell, whose wife had breast cancer, wanted to continue his and his wife's insurance. He was told that it would be continued. McDowell signed a release form waiving all claims related to his employment against either the chiropractic center or Krawchison individually. Half a year later, McDowell's wife sought preapproval for medical treatment and was told that she had no insurance coverage. McDowell and his wife sued Krawchison and the chiropractic corporation alleging violation of COBRA. The court found that the spouse's right to notice was violated since only her husband had received notice. (The court declined to address the issue of whether oral notice was sufficient to McDowell.) The court found that Krawchison was the plan sponsor and individually liable for the failure to give COBRA notice to the qualified beneficiary based on the following reasons:

- Krawchison was the sole owner and officer of most of the clinics and the single common link among all of them.
- He chose to aggregate the clinics' work forces instead of obtaining insurance separately for each clinic.
- The policy was put in his own name rather than in any clinic-employer's name.
- Evidence showed that he made decisions regarding the plan's administration.

State Coverage

In addition to the federal COBRA statute, employers should be aware of their own state COBRA laws. For instance, New York law provides that coverage must be continued for a minimum of 36 months in the case of the employee's death, divorce, or legal separation and for 18 months minimum coverage in the case of job termination.[159]

CAFETERIA PLANS

Cafeteria plans permit employees to set aside pretax dollars to purchase qualified benefits.[160] Cafeteria plans (also termed *flexible benefits plans*), permit an employee to choose from a selection of benefits. This approach gives the employee an individually tailored benefits package and provides the employer with the potential for lowered costs and increased employee morale. Requirements of a cafeteria plan are that it is a written plan, all participants must be employees, and it must offer two or more benefits consisting of cash and qualified benefits.[161] In general, benefits that are excludable from the gross income of an employer under a specific section of the U.S.C. may be offered. This excludes scholarships, fellowships, vanpooling, educational assistance, and meals and lodging furnished for the employer's convenience. Benefits that may be offered in a cafeteria plan include the following:

- coverage for group term life insurance up to $50,000,[162] as well as group term life insurance that is includible in gross income either because the coverage is greater than $50,000 or because it is on the lives of a spouse and/or children[163]
- accident coverage[164]
- health coverage[165]
- group legal service plan coverage[166]
- dependent care assistance[167]
- educational assistance[168]
- participation in a qualified cash or deferred arrangement that is part of a profit-sharing or stock bonus plan (401k plan)

- paid vacation days under certain conditions[169]

These benefits are subject to nondiscrimination testing.[170]

Types of Cafeteria Plans

There are a number of choices to be made in the type of cafeteria plan offered. Cafeteria plans include core-plus plans, modular plans, payroll deduction, salary reduction plans, premium conversion plans, and flexible spending accounts. In core-plus plans, the employee can purchase benefits in addition to the basic ones given as part of the employer's benefit package. These additional benefits may be purchased with either dollars or credits given as part of the benefits package. In modular plans, the employer offers a selection of predesigned benefits packages. A basic package will not cost the employee any money, but the employee will contribute to the cost of a more expensive benefits package that provides more extensive benefits. After-tax payroll deductions can be used to purchase benefits in excess of the employer's contribution. In a premium conversion plan, before-tax salary reductions are used to pay for premiums for coverage exceeding what the employer offers in its benefits package. (An advantage to a before-tax salary reduction is that it reduces the amount of taxable income.) In a flexible spending arrangement (FSA), the participant uses pretax dollars to pay for medical[171] or dependent care expenses. Incurred expenses are reimbursed subject to a maximum amount that cannot exceed the amount paid for premium coverage by both the employer and the employee. The total reimbursement amount is available at any time during the coverage period.[172] Salary reduction has many implications for a health care employee, which the benefits administrator should discuss with potential participants. Unused money remaining in an FSA is forfeited by the employee, so the amount authorized should be carefully and realistically figured. Since a salary reduction reduces the employee's salary, it affects an employee's Social Security and other benefits that base benefits on actual salary. The employee's credit eligibility can also be affected by the salary reduction.

Administering Cafeteria Plans

The health care administrator needs to have a set of administrative rules in place in order to effectively, efficiently, and correctly administer cafeteria-style benefits plans. These plans are particularly challenging because employees will choose different levels of coverage and benefits. The rules should be analyzed annually to ensure that they cover all situations. The annual enrollment process is the time when the benefits personnel must provide all of the information regarding the available benefits. At this time, the benefits personnel will collect the employees' data, prepare and distribute the individual enrollment forms based on that data, collect the completed forms, check them for correct elections based on the amount of flexible dollars an employee had to spend, and send confirmations to the participants.

Prepaid Legal Services

Prepaid legal services are a welcome benefit because they enable an employee to hire a lawyer without the high cost traditionally associated with legal work. A qualified group legal services plan is a separate written plan for the exclusive benefit of the participating employee, spouse, and dependents to provide them with personal legal services. This benefit is excluded from gross income. The plan is subject to discrimination testing, and the benefits administrator must be sure that the plan does not favor highly compensated employees. Employees who are not included in the plan but who are part of the collective bargaining unit are excluded in the discrimination testing if prepaid legal services were a subject of good faith bargaining.

Prepaid legal services are subject to ERISA requirements because they fall into the category of an "employee welfare benefit plan."[173] There is a choice between open- or closed-panel formats. In an open panel, the participant is free to choose an attorney from all the local lawyers in the plan. In a closed panel, a group of attorneys is selected by the health care organization, and the participant is restricted to using one of these lawyers. Modified plans are also available in which the employee can choose between panel and nonpanel lawyers and is reimbursed a certain percentage of the fee charged by a nonpanel lawyer. When choosing lawyers to be part of the attorney panel from which the participants will select, the benefits administrator should check the lawyers' competency, training, and experience. The benefit is only as good as the legal expertise it offers.[174]

In general, a prepaid legal services contract should be presumed to be reasonable. By accepting a fee schedule of this sort, an attorney agrees that the fee is customary and reasonable as to all persons included. The attorney is not entitled to additional compensation beyond the fee schedule.[175]

Dependent Care Assistance

Dependent care assistance is a separate written plan, and reasonable notice of its availability and terms must be given to all employees. It is subject to discrimination testing, and, generally, a plan meets the requirements if the average benefits provided to employees who are not highly compensated employees under all plans of the employer are at least 55 percent of the average benefits provided to highly compensated employees under all plans of the employer. Employees under the age of 21 who have not completed a year of service and employees who are not participating in the plan but who are part of a collective bargaining unit in which dependent care assistance was the subject of good faith bargaining are excluded from discrimination testing. By January 31 of every plan year, each participant must be given a written statement showing the amounts paid or expenses incurred by the employer in providing dependent care assistance.[176]

Educational Assistance Benefits

An educational assistance benefit[177] is a sought-after benefit because education is expensive. The employer benefits because its employees are able to take training courses, workshops, or courses toward degrees, resulting in increased skills. Educational assistance benefits are deducted as a business expense. Whether the course is job related or not, the employee can deduct at least part of its expense from gross income as a working condition fringe benefit. If the education is job related,[178] then there is no limit to the deduction, whereas if it is not, the deduction is limited.

An educational assistance plan is a separate written benefit for the exclusive use of the employee. Neither spouses nor dependents can participate in this benefit. Educational assistance plans are subject to discrimination testing. However, if the educational assistance benefits were the subject of good faith collective bargaining, then employees within the unit who do not participate are excluded.

Record-Keeping Requirements

The benefits administrator must know the federal filing requirements and keep all records for tax years in which these benefits are excludable from gross income. The statute provides that the employer is required to file a return for participants that includes the following information:[179]

1. the number of employees of the employer
2. the number of employees of the employer eligible to participate under the plan
3. the number of employees participating under the plan
4. the total cost of the plan during the year
5. the name, address, and taxpayer identification number of the employer and the type of business in which the employer is engaged
6. the number of highly compensated employees among the employees described in 1, 2, and 3.

The employer is also required to keep records that may be necessary to determine whether the exclusion's requirements are met. The IRS may request this information, and the benefits administrator should be sure that pertinent records are maintained. If the plan is a multiemployer plan, then the plan will be required to provide this information if the agreement between the plan and the employer indicates that the plan is responsible for maintaining these records.

PERSONAL SERVICES BENEFITS

Personal services benefits can make life easier for the employee and therefore increase productivity and job satisfaction, resulting ultimately in a boon for the employer. Personal services benefits are tailored to the needs of the organization's work force and are usually a reflection of it. These benefits include work/family and convenience benefits.

Work/Family

Work/family benefits seek to ease the burden of balancing work and family responsibilities. They are offered to all employees regardless of rank. Work/family personal service benefits range from the company giving a new parent a savings bond on the birth of a child, free summer camp, private tutoring, a cash gift at high school graduation, tuition assistance for college, 24-hour on-site child care, sick child care, and on-site schools. The long shifts worked by health care employees make 24-hour on-site child care, sick child care, and on-site schools particularly useful benefits. At the other end of the life cycle is the need to care for aging parents. On-site older adult day care facilities is a benefit that is really appreciated by a work force. A health care organization is well set up to care for older people and may be able to use facilities already in place and just extend the use of the facility to the parents of the employees. The benefits administrator should be aware that an inferior facility will damage the employer's reputation and could lead to personal liability issues. These facilities must be licensed and monitored by the employer.[180] However, at the least, if it is not economically justifiable to actually care for young children and older adults on site, the human resource professional can offer a referral service to licensed facilities through the use of an employee assistance program. Employee assistance programs help the employee locate telephone referral services for employees needing legal advice; babysitters; help with teenage children; help with family finances; and, ever important, referrals for social services for employees who are domestic violence victims or drug/alcohol abusers.

Flex Time

Flex time is a very popular benefit that meets the needs of both the health care organizations and the employees. Flex time allows employees to arrange their work schedules to fit their own responsibilities. Health care organizations can arrange shifts to fit the needs of the employers, the employees, and the customer. Parents who need to see children off to school may prefer to arrange their schedule to work at night, start work at 9:30 AM, or even work a compressed schedule during four days and nights and have off for three days. While the benefits manager must be concerned with cost containment, these benefits have been proven to add to the substantive quality of the workplace and are well worth their monetary cost.

Convenience Benefits

Convenience benefits relieve employees' stress by providing them with efficient ways to deal with the demands on them. Convenience benefits include on-site grocery shopping, concierge services for all types of errands as varied as bringing shoes to a shoe repair shop to taking an employee's car to the service station, on-site medical care, on-site dry cleaners, emergency home repair services, membership discounts in health clubs, warehouse grocery stores, and taxi or limousine services for employees working odd hours and second shifts as is so often the situation in the health care industry. Parking spaces, cafeterias, snack bars, and the like are in a sense fringe benefits for the employee, all of which makes for more satisfied, efficient, and permanent employees.[181]

On-site medical care is typically given as a benefit by health care organizations. It can reduce the use of sick days and personal days taken to see a physician.[182] Free or reduced membership in a health club reflects the health care organization's concern with wellness. Other personal service benefits that can be offered by a health care organization include access to blood banks and prescription plans for the employee and family.

MERGERS AND ACQUISITIONS

Health care organizations are subject to restructuring, particularly by mergers, joint ventures, and buy-outs. These occur between all combinations of nonprofit and for-profit organizations. Other business restructuring takes place when affiliated service groups are created. The merger plan must offer all of the benefits, rights, and features that have already accrued under the plan that is merging in. A reduction of benefits not yet accrued is permissible if 15 days written notice is given. Participants in benefit welfare plans whose benefits may be affected by corporate reorganization are entitled to bring suit under ERISA 510.[183]

CONCLUSION

Employee benefits make up a significant portion of an employee's compensation package. Employees expect to receive certain benefits, and for employers to stay competitive in these days of full employment, they must be offered. However, human resource personnel should weigh the actual benefit against the cost. Although eliminating costly benefits may not be practical, resourceful methods of providing those benefits should be used. In fact, personal service benefits are not costly, but are a proven way to maintain a satisfied work force. Personnel must also be sure to stay current with legal regulations and to know their own state's laws.

NOTES

1. Vizcaino v. Microsoft Corp., 120 F.3d 1006 (9th Cir. 1997).
2. Vizcaino v. Microsoft Corp., 120 F.3d 1006 (9th Cir. 1997).
3. 26 U.S.C. §§ 132(h); 401(k)(5); 414(q); 505(b)(5).
4. 26 U.S.C. § 105(h).
5. Turner v. Fallon Comm. Health Plan, Inc., No. 97-1253 (1st Cir. Oct. 20, 1997).

6. Shaw v. Delta Air Lines, Inc., 463 U.S. 85 (1983).

7. Note that apprenticeship and day care centers established by the employer are exempt from most ERISA reporting requirements. DOL Reg. 2520 104-22(a), 104-25.

8. 29 U.S.C. § 1002(1).

9. Swinney v. General Motors Corp., 46 F.3d 512 (6th Cir. 1995).

10. Gahn v. Allstate Life Ins. Co., 926 F.2d 1449 (5th Cir. 1991).

11. 29 C.F.R. § 2510.3-1(j).

12. Taggart Corp. v. Efros, 617 F.2d 1208 (5th Ct. 1980), *cert. denied*, 450 U.S. 1030 (1980).

13. Hansen v. Continental Ins. Co., 940 F.2d 971 (5th Cir. 1991).

14. 29 U.S.C. § 1022(a)(1).

15. If plan participants do not read English and do read the same foreign language, then the SPD must be accompanied by a notice written in their language that assistance is available to help them understand their rights. 29 USC § 1024(b)(1). The foreign language notice applies as follows: If the plan covers fewer than 100 participants at the beginning of the plan year, then 25% or more must be literate only in the same foreign language; if the plan covers 100 or more participants at the beginning of the plan year, then only if: 500 or more participants are literate only in the same language, or at least 10% of the plan participants are literate only in the same language. DOL Reg. § 2520.102-2(c)(1),(2).

16. 29 U.S.C. § 1024(b)(1)(A),(B).

17. Hein v. TechAmerica Group, 17 F.3d 1278 (10th Cir. 1994).

18. 29 U.S.C. § 1022 and 29 C.F.R. § 2520.102-3.

19. In Doe v. Travellers Insurance Co., 971 F. Supp. 623 (D.C. Mass. 1997), the plaintiff's claim was rejected, and during the appeal process, she requested a copy of the medical reviewers report, which had been the basis of the decision. The defendant insurance company did not provide the plaintiff with the Medical Necessity Guidelines she had requested claiming that the request was vague. The court found that although the plaintiff did not and, of course, could not identify the specific documents she was requesting, her request was clear and that the refusal was unfair, making the decision to deny benefits arbitrary and capricious.

20. 29 U.S.C. § 1341(c)(1); Meyers Moving & Storage v. Michigan Life & Health Ins. Guaranty Ass., 566 N.W.2d 632 (Mich. Ct. App. 1997).

21. 29 C.F.R. §§ 2606, 2616, 2617, 2629.

22. IRS Revenue Ruling 76-378, IRB 1976-40.

23. See section on HIPAA.

24. *See* Pierce v. Security Trust Life Ins. Co., 979 F.2d 23 (4th Cir. 1992), finding that if the SPD favors the employees, it can be relied on despite the disclaimer, and *see also* Glocker v. WR Grace & Co., 974 F.2d 540 (4th Cir. 1992), holding that if the SPD favors the employer, and the plan favors the participants, the disclaimer will be relied on.

25. McKnight v. Southern Life & Health Ins. Co., 758 F.2d 1566 (11th Cir. 1985) reliance required: "It is of no effect to publish and distribute a SPD de-

signed to simplify and explain a voluminous and complex document and then proclaim that any inconsistencies will be governed by the plan." Similarly, Govoni v. Bricklayers, Masons & Plasterers Int'l Union, 732 F.2d 250 (1st Cir. 1984); not required: Edwards v. State Farm Mutual Auto Ins. Co., 851 F.2d 134 (6th Cir. 1988).

26. Andersen v. Chrysler Corp., 99 F.3d 846 (7th Cir. 1996); Panaras v. Liquid Carbonic Indus. Corp., 74 F.3d 786 (7th Cir. 1996), *reh'g denied*, No. 95-1784 (1996); Meredith v. Allsteel, Inc., 11 F.3d 1354 (7th Cir. 1993), *reh'g denied*, 92-3997 (1994) *mot. granted*, 92 C 1856 (1994), *overruled on other grounds*, Ahng v. Allsteel, Inc. 96 F.3d 1033 (7th Cir. 1996).

27. Hicks v. Fleming Cos., 961 F.2d 537 (5th Cir. 1992), *aff'g*, 802 F. Supp. 39 (S.D. Tex. 1991).

28. Kochendorfer v. Rockdale Sash & Trim Co., Inc., 653 F. Supp. 612 (N.D. Ill. 1987).

29. Gridley v. Cleveland Pneumatic Co., 924 F.2d 1310 (3d Cir. 1991), *cert denied*, 501 U.S. 1232 (1991).

30. Copying fees of up to .25 per page can be charged for all these documents except the annual benefit statement. ERISA § 105(a); DOL Reg § 2520-104b-30.

31. 29 U.S.C. §§ 1001(b), 1132(a)(1)(B); Howard v. Gleason Corp., 901 F.2d 1154 (2d Cir. 1990), *aff'g*, 716 F. Supp. 740 (W.D.N.Y. 1989).

32. This pertains to changes made on or after the first day of the first plan year beginning after June 30, 1997.

33. Interim Rules, 62 Fed. Reg. 16894 (April 8, 1997).

34. 29 U.S.C. § 1024(b)(1); DOL Reg § 2520.104.b-3.

35. Fort Halifax Packing Co., Inc., v. Coyne, 482 U.S. 1 (1987).

36. 29 U.S.C. § 1144(a). Shaw v. Delta Air Lines, 463 U.S. 85 (1983). ERISA's savings clause is found at 29 U.S.C. 1144(6)(A).

37. Ingersoll-Rand Co. v. McClendon, 498 U.S. 133 (1990); 29 U.S.C. § 1144(c)(1).

38. Nazay v. Miller, 949 F.2d 1323 (3d Cir. 1991).

39. Pacificare of Oklahoma, Inc. v. Burrage, 59 F.3d 151 (10th Cir. 1991).

40. NYS Conference of Blue Cross/Blue Shield Plans v. Travelers Ins. Co., 514 U.S. 645 (1995).

41. American Medical Soc. v. Bartlett, 111 F.3d 358 (4th Cir. 1997), *petition for cert. filed* (Aug. 4, 1997) and later proceeding, Larsen v. American Med. Soc., 66 U.S.L.W. 3336 (1997).

42. Kearney v. U.S. Healthcare, Inc., 859 F. Supp.182 (E.D. Pa. 1994), citing Kuhl v. Lincoln Nat. Health Plan, 999 F.2d 298 (8th Cir.1993), *cert. denied*, 510 U.S. 1045 (1994) (claims for breach of contract and malpractice against plan administrator for delaying heart surgery arose from administration of benefits and preempted; Elsesser v. Hospital of Philadelphia College, 802 F. Supp.1286 (E.D. Pa. 1992) claims against plan adminstrator for wrongful refusal to pay for testing and for breach of contractual obligations and misrepresentation regarding qualifications of primary care physicians and availability of specialized treatment preempted. A claim based on negligent failure to de-

termine a dentist's competence and misrepresenting the benefits offered was preempted. Altieri v. CIGNA Dental Health, Inc., 753 F. Supp. 61 (D. Conn. 1990).

43. Wilson v. Zoellner, 114 F.2d 713 (8th Cir. 1997).

44. Barnes v. Lacy, 927 F.2d 539 (11th Cir. 1991).

45. Payonk v. HMW Industries, Inc. 883 F.2d 221 (3d Cir. 1989).

46. Baxter v. C.A. Muer Corp., 941 F.2d 451 (6th Cir. 1991), *reh'g, en banc denied,* No. 90-1806 (6th Cir. Sept. 24 1991).

47. Amato v. Western Union, Inc. 773 F.2d 1402 (2d Cir. 1985), *cert. dis.,* 474 U.S. 1113 (1986).

48. Campbell v. Aerospace Corp., 123 F.3d 1308 (9th Cir. 1997). *See also* WSB Elec. Inc. v. Curry, 88 F.3d 788 (1996).

49. Sejman v. Warner-Lambert Co., Inc., 889 F.2d 1346 (4th Cir. 1989), *reh'g denied,* Nos. 88-2606, 88-2607 (4th Cir. Jan. 5), *cert. denied,* 498 U.S. 810 (1990).

50. Young v. Standard Oil, 849 F.2d 1039 (7th Cir. 1988), *cert. denied,* 488 U.S. 981 (1988).

51. Six Clinics Holding Corp. v. Cafcomp Systems, Inc., 119 F.3d 393 (6th Cir. 1997).

52. Haberern v. Kaupp Vascular Surgeons Ltd. Defined Benefit Pension Plan, 24 F.3d 1491 (3d Cir. Pa. 1994), *reh'g, en banc denied,* No. 93-1892 (3d Cir.), *cert. denied,* 513 U.S. 1149, *mot. granted in part, mot. denied in part,* Civil Action 88-1853 (E.D. Pa.), *appeal,* 65 F.3d 162 (3d Cir. Pa.1995).

53. Amato v. Western Union Inter., Inc., 773 F.2d 1402 (2d Cir. 1985) *cert. denied,* Western Union International, Inc. v. Amato, 474 U.S. 1113 (1986).

54. Geller v. County Line Auto Sales, 86 F.3d 18 (2d Cir.), *on remand, claim dismissed,* CV-94-3123 (E.D.N.Y. 1996).

55. Pompano v. Schiavone & Sons, Inc., 680 F.2d 911 (2d Cir.), *cert. denied,* 459 U.S. 1039 (1982).

56. Varity v. Howe, 516 U.S. 489 (1996).

57. 29 U.S.C. § 1002(2)(A).

58. 29 U.S.C. § 1001(a).

59. 26 U.S.C. §§ 83, 162, 402(b), 404.

60. IRS Notice of 97-6 (Jan. 13, 1996) & Rev. Proc. 97-9 (Jan. 13, 1997).

61. 26 U.S.C. §§ 401(a)(1); 401(a)(2). There are many other requirements for a qualified retirement plan.

62. Profit-sharing plans include employee contributions, IRAs, employee after-tax contributions, employee 401(k) pretax salary deferrals, and employee 401(k) matching contributions.

63. Note that welfare benefit plans are not subject to vesting. United Paperworkers Int'l Union v. Jefferson Smurfit Corp. 961 F.2d 1384 (8th Cir. 1992); *See also* Unisys Corp. v. Retiree Medical Benefits "ERISA" Litigation, 58 F.3d 896 (3rd Cir. 1995), *cert. denied,* Unisys Corp. v. Pickering, 134 L. Ed. 2d 470 (1996).

64. 29 U.S.C. § 1053.

65. 29 U.S.C. § 1053(B).

66. Treas Reg § 1.401-1(b)(2).

67. Exclusions include union employees if retirement benefits were the subject of "good faith" bargaining, 26 U.S.C. § 410(b)(3); classification by job description, geographic location, specific division of the company, and hourly or salaried employees, 26 U.S.C. §§ 401(a)26, 410(b).

68. 26 U.S.C. § 410(b)(3).

69. The SBJPA of '96 modified many aspects of pension law.

70. 26 U.S.C. § 6058.

71. 60 Fed. Reg. 20874.

72. 26 U.S.C. §§ 83, 402(b).

73. 26 U.S.C. § 401(a).

74. American Drug Stores v. Harvard Pilgrim Health Care, Inc. 973 F. Supp. 60 (D.C. Mass. 1997).

75. See e.g. Mass. Gen. Law Ch. 176D (3)(B).

76. DOL is considering extending the rule to other plans, including pension plans, and to other plan disclosures, but is exploring whether special precautions are necessary to ensure the confidentiality of electronically transmitted individual account or benefit-related information. Pension and Welfare Benefits Programs, ERISA Technical Release No. 96-1.

77. Shaw v. Delta Air Lines, Inc., 463 U.S. 85 (1983).

78. Metropolitan Life Ins. Co. v. Mass., 471 U.S. 724 (1985).

79. McGann v. H & H Music, Inc., 946 F.2 401 (5th Cir. 1991), *mot. granted*, Greenberg v. H & H Music Co., 503 U.S. 958, *cert. denied*, 506 U.S. 981 (1992). *See also* Owens v. Storehouse, Inc., 984 F.2d 394 (11th Cir. 1993).

80. NMHPA does not have a separate effective date for collectively bargained plans.

81. 29 U.S.C. § 1169(a)(3)(a).

82. These are accident insurance, disability insurance, liability insurance, workers' compensation, automobile medical insurance, credit insurance, on-site medical clinics, long-term care insurance, specific disease insurance, fixed indemnity insurance, Medicare supplement insurance, and military health care supplemental insurance.

83. Interim Rules, 62 Fed. Reg. 16894.

84. As of this writing, no state had done so.

85. Lutheran Hospital of Indiana, Inc. v. Business Men's Assur. Co. of America, 51 F.3d 1308 (7th Cir. 1995); COBRA amendments to ERISA are found at 29 U.S.C. §§ 1161–1168.

86. H.R. Rep. No. 241, Part 1, 99th Congr., 2d Sess. 44. For a general discussion of COBRA, *see* Gaskell v. Harvard Coop. Soc., 3 F.3d 495 (1st Cir. 1993).

87. 29 U.S.C. § 1162(1); Lutheran Hosp. of Indiana, Inc. v. Business Men's Assur. Co. of America, 51 F.3d 1308 (7th Cir. 1995).

88. Austell v. Raymond James & Assoc., Inc., 120 F.3d 32 (4th Cir. 1997).

89. Jefferson v. Reliance Standard Life Ins. Co., 818 F. Supp. 1523 (M.D. Fla. 1993).

90. Defined in 29 U.S.C. § 1002(32).

91. Defined in 29 U.S.C. § 1002(33).

92. 29 U.S.C. § 1161.

93. An employee organization may also be subject to COBRA regulations if it provides health benefits to its members. 26 U.S.C. § 4980B(g)(2), 50000(b)(1), as amended by OBRA '93, § 13561(e)(2)(A)(ii).

94. Local 217, Hotel & Restaurant Employees Union v. MHM, Inc., 976 F.2d 805 (2d Cir. 1992), citing S.R. 99-146, 99th Cong., reprinted in 1986 U.S.C.C.A.N. 42.

95. 29 U.S.C. § 1161(b).

96. Johnson v. Reserve Life Ins. Co., 765 F. Supp. 1478 (D.C. Cal. 1991).

97. Kidder v. H & B Marine, Inc., 734 F. Supp. 724 (E.D. La. 1990), *aff'd*, 925 F.2d 857, *aff'd in part, rev'd in part on other grounds*, 932 F.2d 347 (5th Cir. 1991); Martinez v. Dodge Printing Centers, Inc., 123 B.R. 77 (Colo. 1991).

98. Martinez v. Dodge Printing Centers, 123 B.R. 77 (Colo. 1991).

99. This is a qualifying event for the beneficiaries only and not for the covered employee. 26 U.S.C. § 4980B(g)(1); ERISA § 607(3)(B); Prop. Treas. Reg. § 1.62-26, Q&A-15[c].

100. 29 U.S.C. 1167; 26 U.S.C. § 4980B(f)(6)(B). However, usually beneficiaries do not lose coverage as a result of the active employee's Medicare entitlement. Medicare entitlement only triggers COBRA rights if it causes the qualified beneficiary to lose coverage under a group health plan. Otherwise, Medicare entitlement does not count as a qualifying event. 26 U.S.C. § 4980B(f)(3); Prop. Treas. Reg. § 1.162-26, Q&A-18(c). COBRA benefits can be terminated for beneficiaries with end-stage renal disease who are entitled to Medicare; 42 C.F.R. § 411.100-411.162; Blue Cross and Blue Shield of Texas v. Shalala, 995 F.2d 70 (5th Cir. 1993).

101. Mlsna v. Unitel Communications, 41 F.3d 1124 (7th Cir. 1994), *reh'g denied*, No. 94-1477 (7th Cir. Jan. 5, 1995), appeal after remand, 91 F.3d 876 (7th Cir. 1996).

102. Aquilera v. Landmark Hotel-Metairie & Ben Resources, Inc., 92-1815 (E.D. La. 1992).

103. Conery v. Bath Assoc., 803 F. Supp. 1388 (N.D. Ind. 1992).

104. Paris v. F. Korbel & Bros., Inc., 751 F. Supp. 838 (N.D. Cal. 1990), (basing the definition of gross misconduct on state law).

105. Burke v. American Stores, Inc., Employee Benefit Plan, 818 F. Supp. 1131 (N.D. Ill. 1993).

106. Collins v. Aggreko, Inc., 884 F. Supp. 450 (D.C. Utah 1995).

107. OBRA '89.

108. 26 U.S.C. § 4980B(f)(6).

109. 26 U.S.C. § 4980B(f)(2)(B)(i)(v).

110. 62 Fed. Reg. 16894 (April 8, 1997).

111. 26 U.S.C. § 4980B(f)(3)(F), (g)(1)(D).

112. Kidder v. H & B Marine, Inc., 734 F. Supp. 724 (E.D. La. 1990), *aff'd in part, rev'd in part on other grounds*, 932 F.2d 347 (5th Cir. 1991).

113. McDowell v. Krawchison, 125 F.2d 954 (6th Cir. 1997). *See also* Smith v. Rogers Galvanizing Co., 96-5168 (10 Cir. 1997).

114. See section on SPD distribution.

115. Mlsna v. Unitel Communications, 41 F.3d 1124 (7th Cir. 1994), *reh'g denied,* No. 94-1477 (7th Cir. Jan. 5, 1995), appeal after remand, 91 F.3d 876 (7th Cir. 1996); Phillips v. Riverside, Inc., 796 F. Supp. 403 (E.D. Ark. 1992).

116. This includes the death of a retired employee, an agent, an independent contractor, a corporate director, and a self-employed person. 26 U.S.C. § 4980B(f)(7).

117. 26 U.S.C. § 4980B(f)(6)(B).

118. Kidder v. H & B Marine, Inc., 734 F. Supp. 724 (La. 1990), *aff'd,* 925 F.2d 857, *op withdrawn, substituted op,* 932 F.2d 347 (5th Cir. 1991). *See also* Ward v. Bethenergy Mines, 851 F. Supp. 235 (S.D. W.Va. 1994).

119. 1995 ERISA LEXIS 18 (Apr. 11, 1995). This is an Information Letter issued by the DOL.

120. For example, Mlsna, 825 F. Supp. 862, found that COBRA requires separate notice to both the employee and spouse; while Conery v. Bath Assoc's., 803 F. Supp. 1388 (N.D. Ind. 1992) found that notice to a covered employee is sufficient notice to all other qualified beneficiaries at the same last known address. Dehner v. Kansas City Southern Indus., Inc., 713 F. Supp. 1397 (D. Kan. 1989) held that including the spouse and the employee's notification in the same envelope with instructions to the employee to give the notice to the spouse was sufficient under COBRA.

121. Van Hoove v. Mid-Atlantic Building Maintenance, Inc., 841 F. Supp. 1523 (1993), *motion granted in part,* Civ. No. 90-1068-FGT (D. Kan. March 30, 1994).

122. 26 U.S.C. § 4980B(f)(6)(C).

123. Van Hoove v. Mid-Atlantic Building Maintenance, Inc., 841 F. Supp. 1523 (1993), *motion granted in part,* Civ. No. 90-1068-FGT (D. Kan. March 30, 1994).

124. Jachim v. KUTV, Inc., 783 F. Supp. 1328 (D.C. Utah 1992).

125. Lincoln General Hospital v. Blue Cross/Blue Shield of Nebraska, 963 F.2d 1136 (8th Cir. 1992), *reh'g on banc denied,* No. 91-1777NEL (8th Cir. June 24, 1992).

126. Martin v. Marriott Corp., Civ. No. 91-2289 (D.C. Col. April 10, 1992).

127. Myers v. King's Daughters Clinics, 912 F. Supp. 233 (W.D. Tex. 1996).

128. Phillips v. Riverside, Inc., 796 F. Supp. 403 (E.D. Ark. 1992).

129. 29 U.S.C. § 1059; *See e.g.* Stanton v. Larry Fowler Trucking, Inc., 52 F.3d 723 (8th Cir. 1995).

130. McDowell v. Krawchison, 125 F.3d 954 (6th Cir. 1997).

131. Van Hoove v. Mid-Atlantic Building Maintenance, Inc., 841 F. Supp. 1523 (1993), *motion granted in part,* Civ. No. 90-1068-FGT (D. Kan. March 30, 1994).

132. 26 U.S.C. § 4980B(c)(3)(A)(B).

133. 26 U.S.C. § 4980B(c)(1).

134. 26 U.S.C. §§ 4980(B)(f)(5)(A)(i),(ii),(iii).

135. Nat'l. Cos. Health Benefit Plan v. St. Joseph's Hospital, 928 F.2d 1558 (11th Cir. 1991).

136. Branch v. G. Bernd Co., 764 F. Supp. 1527 (M.D. Ga. 1991), *aff'd*, 955 F.2d 1574 (11th Cir. 1992).

137. Lincoln General Hos. v. Blue Cross/Blue Shield of Nebraska, 963 F.2d 1136 (8th Cir. 1991).

138. 29 U.S.C. § 1165(2); Prop. Treas. Reg. 1-62-26, Q&A-37, 52 Fed. Reg. 22716, 22730 (1987). McDowell v. Krawchison, 125 F.3d 954 (6th Cir. 1997).

139. Noncore coverage includes vision and dental benefits, but vision procedures that must be performed by a physician pursuant to local law are part of core benefits. Dental procedures performed due to accidental injury are core benefits. Prop. Treas. Reg. §§ 1.162-26 Q&A-25(a), (b), (c).

140. It has been held that the 36-month coverage is not available if either both qualifying events are reduction in hours, or reduction in hours is the initial event, and termination is the second event. *See* Burgess v. Adams Tool & Engineering, Inc., 908 F. Supp. 473 (W.D. Mich. 1995).

141. 29 U.S.C. § 1162(2)(A). The SSA's determination of disability may be attacked by the plan administrator. Martin v. Ingersoll-Rand Co., 2:93-CV-169-WCO (N.D. Ga. 1995), *aff'd*, 107 F.3d 25 (11th Cir. 1997). The DOL is inquiring into problems covered employees, qualified beneficiaries, employers, or plan administrators have encountered in obtaining the 11-month extension or in administering the provisions granting the right to the 11-month extension.

142. Remember that Medicare eligibility is a qualifying event for beneficiaries but not for the covered employee. 26 U.S.C. § 4980B(g)(1); ERISA § 607(3)(B); Prop. Treas. Reg. § 1.62-26, Q&A-15[c].

143. 26 U.S.C. § 4980B(f)2(B)(ii); ERISA § 602(2)(B).

144. The coverage must be a group health plan and not an individual insurance policy. Fosso v. State Farm Mutual Automobile Ins. Co., 940 F.2d 388 (8th Cir. 1991).

145. *In re* Appletree Markets, Inc., 19 F.3d 969 (1994).

146. 26 U.S.C. § 4980(B)(f)(2)(iii).

147. 26 U.S.C. § 4980(B)(f)(2)(C).

148. For example, in Oakley v. City of Longmont, 890 F.2d 1128 (10th Cir. 1989), *cert. denied*, 494 U.S. 1082 (1990), the court found that the COBRA benefits could not be terminated despite the beneficiary's preexisting insurance policy. In Lutheran Hosp. Inc. v. Business Men's Assoc. Co. of America, 51 F.3d 1308 (7th Cir. 1995), the court found that the beneficiary was entitled to the "identical benefits" received before the qualifying event. Therefore, the COBRA rights of a beneficiary with dual coverage before the event could not be terminated prematurely. However, in Geissal v. Moore Medical Corp., 114 F.3d 1458 (8th Cir. 1997), the Geissal court found that since COBRA authorizes the termination of continuation coverage on the day that a former em-

ployee becomes a beneficiary under "any other group health plan," 29 U.S.C. § 1162(2)(D)(i), it is largely irrelevant whether the employee obtained that coverage before or after COBRA rights are activated. Congress's goal was to make affordable health care temporarily available to those who otherwise would find themselves without any health coverage, and, therefore, COBRA allows employers to cancel continuation benefits whenever the purpose underlying the statute is served. Similarly, National Cos. Health Benefit Plan v. St. Joseph's Hosp. Inc., 929 F.2d 1558 (11th Cir. 1991) and Brock v. Primedica Inc., 904 F.2d 295 (5th Cir. 1990) held that beneficiaries with dual coverage were not entitled to COBRA benefits. *But see* Teweleit v. Hartford Life & Accident Ins. Co., 43 F.3d 1005 (5th Cir. 1995); COBRA rights may not be terminated if the second group health insurance plan contains an exclusion, or COBRA rights may not be terminated if the second group health insurance plan contains an exclusion or limitation affecting a preexisting condition. This is to ensure that beneficiaries are covered by a health plan. Furthermore, COBRA rights may not be terminated if a significant gap in coverage would be created. Denying coverage when a gap in coverage would otherwise occur would frustrate the congressional intent in creating COBRA.

149. ERISA § 502(a)(1)(A), (c)(1).

150. *See, e.g.,* Burgess v. Adams Tool & Engineering, Inc., 908 F. Supp. 473 (M.D. Mich.1995); Ward v. Bethenergy Mines, Inc., 851 F. Supp. 235 (S.D. W.Va. 1994); Plotkin v. Bearings, Ltd., 777 F. Supp. 1105 (E.D.N.Y. 1991).

151. Phillips v. Riverside, Inc., 796 F. Supp. 403 (E.D. Ark. 1992); Brown v. Neely Truck Line, Inc., 884 F. Supp. 1534 (M.D. Ala. 1995).

152. Mertens v. Hewitt Assoc., 508 U.S. 248 (1993); Mason Tenders Dist. Council Pension Fund v. Messera, 958 F. Supp. 869 (S.D.N.Y. 1997).

153. 29 U.S.C. §§ 1002(21)(A)(i), (iii).

154. LoPocresti v. Terwillger, 126 F.3d 34 (2d Cir. 1997).

155. 29 C.F.R. § 2509.75-5; Yeseta v. Baima, 837 F.2d 380 (9th Cir. 1988).

156. Mertens v. Hewitt Assoc., 508 U.S. 248 (1993).

157. Bixler v. Central Pennsylvania Teamsters Health & Welfare Fund, 12 F.3d 1292 (3rd Cir. 1993). Switzer v. Wal-Mart Stores, Inc., 52 F.3d 1294 (5th Cir. 1995).

158. McDowell v. Krawchison, 125 F.3d 954 (6th Cir. 1997).

159. NY Ins. Law § 3221(m).

160. 26 U.S.C. 125(d).

161. 26 U.S.C. § 125(d)(1)(A), (B).

162. 26 U.S.C. § 79.

163. Temp. Treas. reg. § 1.125-2T.

164. 26 C.F.R. § 105.

165. 26 C.F.R. § 106.

166. 26 C.F.R. § 120.

167. 26 C.F.R. § 129.

168. 26 C.F.R. § 127.

169. 26 C.F.R. § 1.125-2T (1996).

170. See section on nondiscrimination rules, page 3.

171. Health care spending accounts can be used to pay for deductibles and copayments for covered medical expenses and for miscellaneous health care items, such as hearing aids.

172. 26 U.S.C. § 125; Treas. Reg. §§ 1.125-1,-2.

173. 29 U.S.C. § 1002(1).

174. 26 U.S.C. § 120.

175. Sotolongo v. Brake, 616 So. 2d 413 (Sup. Ct. Fl. 1992).

176. See also 26 U.S.C. § 6051(a)(9).

177. 26 C.F.R. § 127.

178. *Job related* is defined in 26 U.S.C. § 132.

179. 26 U.S.C. § 6039D (1997).

180. Flexible spending accounts (FSAs) and flexible benefit plans set up by the health care employer are complements to these programs and an excellent way to help the employee finance expensive day care by using pretax dollars. Employers do not have to contribute to these plans, and they are not expensive to establish. Dependent care assistance can be offered either as part of a cafeteria plan or as a separate benefit.

181. City of Nashville v. State Bd. of Equalization, 360 S.W.2d 458 (Sup. Ct. Tenn. 1962).

182. See 26 USC § 132(c)(1) on qualified employee discounts. Note that if a health care organization provides discounted on-site medical care, the employer may have established a group health insurance benefit that is subject to COBRA. Prop. Treas. Reg. § 1.162-26 Q&A 7(d).

183. Inter-Modal Rail Employees Assoc. v. Atchison Topeka & Santa Fe Railway Co., 117 S.Ct. 1513, *on remand*, 117 F.3d 1136 (9th Cir. 1997).

Appendix A

Selected Provisions— Health Insurance Portability and Accountability Act

29 U.S.C. § 1181. Increased portability through limitation on preexisting condition exclusions

(a) Limitation on preexisting condition exclusion period; crediting for periods of previous coverage. Subject to subsection (d), a group health plan, and a health insurance issuer offering group health insurance coverage, may, with respect to a participant or beneficiary, impose a preexisting condition exclusion only if—
   (1) such exclusion relates to a condition (whether physical or mental), regardless of the cause of the condition, for which medical advice, diagnosis, care, or treatment was recommended or received within the 6-month period ending on the enrollment date;
   (2) such exclusion extends for a period of not more than 12 months (or 18 months in the case of a late enrollee) after the enrollment date; and
   (3) the period of any such preexisting condition exclusion is reduced by the aggregate of the periods of creditable coverage (if any, as defined in subsection (c)(1)) applicable to the participant or beneficiary as of the enrollment date.

(b) Definitions. For purposes of this part (1) Preexisting condition exclusion.
      (A) In general. The term "preexisting condition exclusion" means, with respect to coverage, a limitation or exclusion of benefits relating to a condi-

tion based on the fact that the condition was present before the date of enrollment for such coverage, whether or not any medical advice, diagnosis, care, or treatment was recommended or received before such date.

(B) Treatment of genetic information. Genetic information shall not be treated as a condition described in subsection (a)(1) in the absence of a diagnosis of the condition related to such information.

(2) Enrollment date. The term "enrollment date" means, with respect to an individual covered under a group health plan or health insurance coverage, the date of enrollment of the individual in the plan or coverage or, if earlier, the first day of the waiting period for such enrollment.

(3) Late enrollee. The term "late enrollee" means, with respect to coverage under a group health plan, a participant or beneficiary who enrolls under the plan other than during—

(A) the first period in which the individual is eligible to enroll under the plan, or

(B) a special enrollment period under subsection (f).

(4) Waiting period. The term "waiting period" means, with respect to a group health plan and an individual who is a potential participant or beneficiary in the plan, the period that must pass with respect to the individual before the individual is eligible to be covered for benefits under the terms of the plan.

(c) Rules relating to crediting previous coverage.

(1) Creditable coverage defined. For purposes of this part, the term "creditable coverage" means, with respect to an individual, coverage of the individual under any of the following:

(A) A group health plan.

(B) Health insurance coverage.

(C) Part A or part B of title XVIII of the Social Security Act.

(D) Title XIX of the Social Security Act, other than coverage consisting solely of benefits under section 1928.
(E) Chapter 55 of title 10, United States Code.
(F) A medical care program of the Indian Health Service or of a tribal organization.
(G) A State health benefits risk pool.
(H) A health plan offered under chapter 89 of title 5, United States Code.
(I) A public health plan (as defined in regulations).
(J) A health benefit plan under section 5(e) of the Peace Corps Act (22 U.S.C. 2504(e)).

Such term does not include coverage consisting solely of coverage of excepted benefits (as defined in section 733(c)).

(2) Not counting periods before significant breaks in coverage.
(A) In general. A period of creditable coverage shall not be counted, with respect to enrollment of an individual under a group health plan, if, after such period and before the enrollment date, there was a 63-day period during all of which the individual was not covered under any creditable coverage.
(B) Waiting period not treated as a break in coverage. For purposes of subparagraph (A) and subsection (d)(4), any period that an individual is in a waiting period for any coverage under a group health plan (or for group health insurance coverage) or is in an affiliation period (as defined in subsection (g)(2)) shall not be taken into account in determining the continuous period under subparagraph (A).

(3) Method of crediting coverage.
(A) Standard method. Except otherwise provided under subparagraph (B), for purposes of applying subsection (a)(3), a group health plan, and a health insurance issuer offering group health insurance coverage, shall count a period of cred-

itable coverage without regard to the specific benefits covered during the period.

(B) Election of alternative method. A group health plan, or a health insurance issuer offering group health insurance coverage, may elect to apply subsection (a)(3) based on coverage of benefits within each of several classes or categories of benefits specified in regulations rather than as provided under subparagraph (A). Such election shall be made on a uniform basis for all participants and beneficiaries. Under such election a group health plan or issuer shall count a period of creditable coverage with respect to any class or category of benefits if any level of benefits is covered within such class or category.

(C) Plan notice. In the case of an election with respect to a group health plan under subparagraph (B) (whether or not health insurance coverage is provided in connection with such plan), the plan shall—

(i) prominently state in any disclosure statements concerning the plan, and state to each enrollee at the time of enrollment under the plan, that the plan has made such election, and

(ii) include in such statements a description of the effect of this election.

(4) Establishment of period. Periods of creditable coverage with respect to an individual shall be established through presentation of certifications described in subsection (e) or in such other manner as may be specified in regulations.

(d) Exceptions.

(1) Exclusion not applicable to certain newborns. Subject to paragraph (4), a group health plan, and a health insurance issuer offering group health insurance coverage, may not impose any preexisting condition exclusion in the case of an individual who, as of the last day

of the 30-day period beginning with the date of birth, is covered under creditable coverage.

(2) Exclusion not applicable to certain adopted children. Subject to paragraph (4), a group health plan, and a health insurance issuer offering group health insurance coverage, may not impose any preexisting condition exclusion in the case of a child who is adopted or placed for adoption before attaining 18 years of age and who, as of the last day of the 30-day period beginning on the date of the adoption or placement for adoption, is covered under creditable coverage. The previous sentence shall not apply to coverage before the date of such adoption or placement for adoption.

(3) Exclusion not applicable to pregnancy. A group health plan, and health insurance issuer offering group health insurance coverage, may not impose any preexisting condition exclusion relating to pregnancy as a preexisting condition.

(4) Loss if break in coverage. Paragraphs (1) and (2) shall no longer apply to an individual after the end of the first 63-day period during all of which the individual was not covered under any creditable coverage.

(e) Certifications and disclosure of coverage.

(1) Requirement for certification of period of creditable coverage.

(A) In general. A group health plan, and a health insurance issuer offering group health insurance coverage, shall provide the certification described in subparagraph (B)—

(i) at the time an individual ceases to be covered under the plan or otherwise becomes covered under a COBRA continuation provision,

(ii) in the case of an individual becoming covered under such a provision, at the time the individual ceases to be covered under such provision, and

(iii) on the request on behalf of an individual made not later than 24 months after the date of cessation of the coverage described in clause (i) or (ii), whichever is later.

The certification under clause (i) may be provided, to the extent practicable, at a time consistent with notices required under any applicable COBRA continuation provision.

(B) Certification. The certification described in this subparagraph is a written certification of—

(i) the period of creditable coverage of the individual under such plan and the coverage (if any) under such COBRA continuation provision, and

(ii) the waiting period (if any) (and affiliation period, if applicable) imposed with respect to the individual for any coverage under such plan.

(C) Issuer compliance. To the extent that medical care under a group health plan consists of group health insurance coverage, the plan is deemed to have satisfied the certification requirement under this paragraph if the health insurance issuer offering the coverage provides for such certification in accordance with this paragraph.

(2) Disclosure of information on previous benefits. In the case of an election described in subsection (c)(3)(B) by a group health plan or health insurance issuer, if the plan or issuer enrolls an individual for coverage under the plan and the individual provides a certification of coverage of the individual under paragraph (1)—

(A) upon request of such plan or issuer, the entity which issued the certification provided by the individual shall promptly disclose to such requesting plan or issuer information on coverage of classes and categories of health benefits available under such entity's plan or coverage, and

(B) such entity may charge the requesting plan or issuer for the reasonable cost of disclosing such information.

(3) Regulations. The Secretary shall establish rules to prevent an entity's failure to provide information under paragraph (1) or (2) with respect to previous coverage of an individual from adversely affecting any subsequent coverage of the individual under another group health plan or health insurance coverage.

(f) Special enrollment periods.

(1) Individuals losing other coverage. A group health plan, and a health insurance issuer offering group health insurance coverage in connection with a group health plan, shall permit an employee who is eligible, but not enrolled, for coverage under the terms of the plan (or a dependent of such an employee if the dependent is eligible, but not enrolled, for coverage under such terms) to enroll for coverage under the terms of the plan if each of the following conditions is met:

(A) The employee or dependent was covered under a group health plan or had health insurance coverage at the time coverage was previously offered to the employee or dependent.

(B) The employee stated in writing at such time that coverage under a group health plan or health insurance coverage was the reason for declining enrollment, but only if the plan sponsor or issuer (if applicable) required such a statement at such time and provided the employee with notice of such requirement (and the consequences of such requirement) at such time.

(C) The employee's or dependent's coverage described in subparagraph (A)—

(i) was under a COBRA continuation provision and the coverage under such provision was exhausted; or

(ii) was not under such a provision and either the coverage was terminated as a result of loss of eligibility for the coverage (including as a result of legal separation, divorce, death, termination of employment, or reduction in the number of hours of employment) or employer contributions toward such coverage were terminated.

(D) Under the terms of the plan, the employee requests such enrollment not later than 30 days after the date of exhaustion of coverage described in subparagraph (C)(i) or termination of coverage or employer contribution described in subparagraph (C)(ii).

(2) For dependent beneficiaries.

(A) In general. If—

(i) a group health plan makes coverage available with respect to a dependent of an individual,

(ii) the individual is a participant under the plan (or has met any waiting period applicable to becoming a participant under the plan and is eligible to be enrolled under the plan but for a failure to enroll during a previous enrollment period), and

(iii) a person becomes such a dependent of the individual through marriage, birth, or adoption or placement for adoption,

the group health plan shall provide for a dependent special enrollment period described in subparagraph (B) during which the person (or, if not otherwise enrolled, the individual) may be enrolled under the plan as a dependent of the individual, and in the case of the birth or adoption of a child, the spouse of the individual may be enrolled as a dependent of the individual if such spouse is otherwise eligible for coverage.

(B) Dependent special enrollment period. A dependent special enrollment period under this subparagraph shall be a period of not less than 30 days and shall begin on the later of—

(i) the date dependent coverage is made available, or

(ii) the date of the marriage, birth, or adoption or placement for adoption (as the case may be) described in subparagraph (A)(iii).

(C) No waiting period. If an individual seeks to enroll a dependent during the first 30 days of such a dependent special enrollment period, the coverage of the dependent shall become effective—

(i) in the case of marriage, not later than the first day of the first month beginning after the date the completed request for enrollment is received;

(ii) in the case of a dependent's birth, as of the date of such birth; or

(iii) in the case of a dependent's adoption or placement for adoption, the date of such adoption or placement for adoption.

(g) Use of affiliation period by HMOs as alternative to preexisting condition exclusion.

(1) In general. In the case of a group health plan that offers medical care through health insurance coverage offered by a health maintenance organization, the plan may provide for an affiliation period with respect to coverage through the organization only if—

(A) no preexisting condition exclusion is imposed with respect to coverage through the organization,

(B) the period is applied uniformly without regard to any health status-related factors, and

(C) such period does not exceed 2 months (or 3 months in the case of a late enrollee).

(2) Affiliation period.

(A) Defined. For purposes of this part, the term "affiliation period" means a period which, under the terms of the health insurance coverage offered by the health maintenance organization, must expire before the health insurance coverage becomes effective. The organization is not required to provide health care services or benefits during such period and no premium shall be charged to the participant or beneficiary for any coverage during the period.

(B) Beginning. Such period shall begin on the enrollment date.

(C) Runs concurrently with waiting periods. An affiliation period under a plan shall run concurrently with any waiting period under the plan.

(3) Alternative methods. A health maintenance organization described in paragraph (1) may use alternative methods, from those described in such paragraph, to address adverse selection as approved by the State insurance commissioner or official or officials designated by the State to enforce the requirements of part A of title XXVII of the Public Health Service Act for the State involved with respect to such issuer.

29 U.S.C. § 1182. Prohibiting discrimination against individual participants and beneficiaries based on health status.

(a) In eligibility to enroll.

(1) In general. Subject to paragraph (2), a group health plan, and a health insurance issuer offering group health insurance coverage in connection with a group health plan, may not establish rules for eligibility (including continued eligibility) of any individual to enroll under the terms of the plan based on any of the following health status-related factors in relation to the individual or a dependent of the individual:

(A) Health status.

(B) Medical condition (including both physical and mental illnesses).

(C) Claims experience.

(D) Receipt of health care.

(E) Medical history.

(F) Genetic information.

(G) Evidence of insurability (including conditions arising out of acts of domestic violence).

(H) Disability.

(2) No application to benefits or exclusions. To the extent consistent with section 701, paragraph (1) shall not be construed—

(A) to require a group health plan, or group health insurance coverage, to provide particular benefits other than those provided under the terms of such plan or coverage, or

(B) to prevent such a plan or coverage from establishing limitations or restrictions on the amount, level, extent, or nature of the benefits or coverage for similarly situated individuals enrolled in the plan or coverage.

(3) Construction. For purposes of paragraph (1), rules for eligibility to enroll under a plan include rules defining any applicable waiting periods for such enrollment.

(b) In premium contributions.

(1) In general. A group health plan, and a health insurance issuer offering health insurance coverage in connection with a group health plan, may not require any individual (as a condition of enrollment or continued enrollment under the plan) to pay a premium or contribution which is greater than such premium or contribution for a similarly situated individual enrolled in the plan on the basis of any health status-related factor in relation to the individual or to an individual enrolled under the plan as a dependent of the individual.

(2) Construction. Nothing in paragraph (1) shall be construed—

(A) to restrict the amount that an employer may be charged for coverage under a group health plan; or

(B) to prevent a group health plan, and a health insurance issuer offering group health insurance coverage, from establishing premium discounts or rebates or modifying otherwise applicable copayments or deductibles in return for adherence to programs of health promotion and disease prevention.

29 U.S.C. § 1183. Guaranteed renewability in multiemployer plans and multiple employer welfare arrangements

A group health plan which is a multiemployer plan or which is a multiple employer welfare arrangement may not deny an employer whose employees are covered under such a plan continued access to the same or different coverage under the terms of such a plan, other than—

(1) for nonpayment of contributions;
(2) for fraud or other intentional misrepresentation of material fact by the employer;
(3) for noncompliance with material plan provisions;
(4) because the plan is ceasing to offer any coverage in a geographic area;
(5) in the case of a plan that offers benefits through a network plan, there is no longer any individual enrolled through the employer who lives, resides, or works in the service area of the network plan and the plan applies this paragraph uniformly without regard to the claims experience of employers or any health status-related factor in relation to such individuals or their dependents; and
(6) for failure to meet the terms of an applicable collective bargaining agreement, to renew a collective bargaining or other agreement requiring or authorizing contributions to the plan, or to employ employees covered by such an agreement.

42 U.S.C. § 300gg. Increased portability through limitation on preexisting condition exclusions

(a) Limitation on preexisting condition exclusion period; crediting for periods of previous coverage. Subject to subsection (d), a group health plan, and a health insurance issuer offering group health insurance coverage, may, with respect to a participant or beneficiary, impose a preexisting condition exclusion only if—
   (1) such exclusion relates to a condition (whether physical or mental), regardless of the cause of the condition, for which medical advice, diagnosis, care, or

treatment was recommended or received within the 6-month period ending on the enrollment date;

(2) such exclusion extends for a period of not more than 12 months (or 18 months in the case of a late enrollee) after the enrollment date; and

(3) the period of any such preexisting condition exclusion is reduced by the aggregate of the periods of creditable coverage (if any, as defined in subsection (c)(1)) applicable to the participant or beneficiary as of the enrollment date.

(b) Definitions. For purposes of this part—

(1) Preexisting condition exclusion.

(A) In general. The term "preexisting condition exclusion" means, with respect to coverage, a limitation or exclusion of benefits relating to a condition based on the fact that the condition was present before the date of enrollment for such coverage, whether or not any medical advice, diagnosis, care, or treatment was recommended or received before such date.

(B) Treatment of genetic information. Genetic information shall not be treated as a condition described in subsection (a)(1) in the absence of a diagnosis of the condition related to such information.

(2) Enrollment date. The term "enrollment date" means, with respect to an individual covered under a group health plan or health insurance coverage, the date of enrollment of the individual in the plan or coverage or, if earlier, the first day of the waiting period for such enrollment.

(3) Late enrollee. The term "late enrollee" means, with respect to coverage under a group health plan, a participant or beneficiary who enrolls under the plan other than during—

(A) the first period in which the individual is eligible to enroll under the plan, or

(B) a special enrollment period under subsection (f).

(4) Waiting period. The term "waiting period" means, with respect to a group health plan and an individual who is a potential participant or beneficiary in the plan, the period that must pass with respect to the individual before the individual is eligible to be covered for benefits under the terms of the plan.

(c) Rules relating to crediting previous coverage.

(1) Creditable coverage defined. For purposes of this title, the term "creditable coverage" means, with respect to an individual, coverage of the individual under any of the following:

(A) A group health plan.

(B) Health insurance coverage.

(C) Part A or part B of title XVIII of the Social Security Act.

(D) Title XIX of the Social Security Act, other than coverage consisting solely of benefits under section 1928.

(E) Chapter 55 of title 10, United States Code.

(F) A medical care program of the Indian Health Service or of a tribal organization.

(G) A State health benefits risk pool.

(H) A health plan offered under chapter 89 of title 5, United States Code.

(I) A public health plan (as defined in regulations).

(J) A health benefit plan under section 5(e) of the Peace Corps Act (22 U.S.C. 2504(e)).

Such term does not include coverage consisting solely of coverage of excepted benefits (as defined in section 2791(c)).

(2) Not counting periods before significant breaks in coverage.

(A) In general. A period of creditable coverage shall not be counted, with respect to enrollment of an individual under a group health plan, if, after such period and before the enrollment date, there was a 63-day period during all of which the individual was not covered under any creditable coverage.

(B) Waiting period not treated as a break in coverage. For purposes of subparagraph (A) and subsection (d)(4), any period that an individual is in a waiting period for any coverage under a group health plan (or for group health insurance coverage) or is in an affiliation period (as defined in subsection (g)(2)) shall not be taken into account in determining the continuous period under subparagraph (A).

(3) Method of crediting coverage.

(A) Standard method. Except as otherwise provided under subparagraph (B), for purposes of applying subsection (a)(3), a group health plan, and a health insurance issuer offering group health insurance coverage, shall count a period of creditable coverage without regard to the specific benefits covered during the period.

(B) Election of alternative method. A group health plan, or a health insurance issuer offering group health insurance, may elect to apply subsection (a)(3) based on coverage of benefits within each of several classes or categories of benefits specified in regulations rather than as provided under subparagraph (A). Such election shall be made on a uniform basis for all participants and beneficiaries. Under such election a group health plan or issuer shall count a period of creditable coverage with respect to any class or category of benefits if any level of benefits is covered within such class or category.

(C) Plan notice. In the case of an election with respect to a group health plan under subparagraph (B) (whether or not health insurance coverage is provided in connection with such plan), the plan shall—

(i) prominently state in any disclosure statements concerning the plan, and state to each enrollee at the time of enrollment under the plan, that the plan has made such election, and

(ii) include in such statements a description of the effect of this election.

(D) Issuer notice. In the case of an election under subparagraph (B) with respect to health insurance coverage offered by an issuer in the small or large group market, the issuer—

(i) shall prominently state in any disclosure statements concerning the coverage, and to each employer at the time of the offer or sale of the coverage, that the issuer has made such election, and

(ii) shall include in such statements a description of the effect of such election.

(4) Establishment of period. Periods of creditable coverage with respect to an individual shall be established through presentation of certifications described in subsection (e) or in such other manner as may be specified in regulations.

(d) Exceptions.

(1) Exclusion not applicable to certain newborns. Subject to paragraph (4), a group health plan, and a health insurance issuer offering group health insurance coverage, may not impose any preexisting condition exclusion in the case of an individual who, as of the last day of the 30-day period beginning with the date of birth, is covered under creditable coverage.

(2) Exclusion not applicable to certain adopted children. Subject to paragraph (4), a group health plan, and a health insurance issuer offering group health insurance coverage, may not impose any preexisting condition exclusion in the case of a child who is adopted or placed for adoption before attaining 18 years of age and who, as of the last day of the 30-day period beginning on the date of the adoption or placement for adoption, is covered under creditable coverage. The previous sentence shall not apply to coverage before the date of such adoption or placement for adoption.

(3) Exclusion not applicable to pregnancy. A group health plan, and health insurance issuer offering group health insurance coverage, may not impose any preexisting condition exclusion relating to pregnancy as a preexisting condition.

(4) Loss if break in coverage. Paragraphs (1) and (2) shall no longer apply to an individual after the end of the first 63-day period during all of which the individual was not covered under any creditable coverage.

(e) Certifications and disclosure of coverage.

(1) Requirement for certification of period of creditable coverage.

(A) In general. A group health plan, and a health insurance issuer offering group health insurance coverage, shall provide the certification described in subparagraph (B)—

(i) at the time an individual ceases to be covered under the plan or otherwise becomes covered under a COBRA continuation provision,

(ii) in the case of an individual becoming covered under such a provision, at the time the individual ceases to be covered under such provision, and

(iii) on the request on behalf of an individual made not later than 24 months after the date of cessation of the coverage described in clause (i) or (ii), whichever is later.

The certification under clause (i) may be provided, to the extent practicable, at a time consistent with notices required under any applicable COBRA continuation provision.

(B) Certification. The certification described in this subparagraph is a written certification of—

(i) the period of creditable coverage of the individual under such plan and the coverage (if any) under such COBRA continuation provision, and

(ii) the waiting period (if any) (and affiliation period, if applicable) imposed with respect to the individual for any coverage under such plan.

(C) Issuer compliance. To the extent that medical care under a group health plan consists of group health insurance coverage, the plan is deemed to have satisfied the certification requirement under this paragraph if the health insurance issuer offering the coverage provides for such certification in accordance with this paragraph.

(2) Disclosure of information on previous benefits. In the case of an election described in subsection (c)(3)(B) by a group health plan or health insurance issuer, if the plan or issuer enrolls an individual for coverage under the plan and the individual provides a certification of coverage of the individual under paragraph (1)—

(A) upon request of such plan or issuer, the entity which issued the certification provided by the individual shall promptly disclose to such requesting plan or issuer information on coverage of classes and categories of health benefits available under such entity's plan or coverage, and

(B) such entity may charge the requesting plan or issuer for the reasonable cost of disclosing such information.

(3) Regulations. The Secretary shall establish rules to prevent an entity's failure to provide information under paragraph (1) or (2) with respect to previous coverage of an individual from adversely affecting any subsequent coverage of the individual under another group health plan or health insurance coverage.

(f) Special enrollment periods.

(1) Individuals losing other coverage. A group health plan, and a health insurance issuer offering group health insurance coverage in connection with a group health plan, shall permit an employee who is eligible, but not enrolled, for coverage under the terms of the plan (or a dependent of such an employee if the dependent is eligible, but not enrolled, for coverage under such

terms) to enroll for coverage under the terms of the plan if each of the following conditions is met:

(A) The employee or dependent was covered under a group health plan or had health insurance coverage at the time coverage was previously offered to the employee or dependent.

(B) The employee stated in writing at such time that coverage under a group health plan or health insurance coverage was the reason for declining enrollment, but only if the plan sponsor or issuer (if applicable) required such a statement at such time and provided the employee with notice of such requirement (and the consequences of such requirement) at such time.

(C) The employee's or dependent's coverage described in subparagraph (A)—

   (i) was under a COBRA continuation provision and the coverage under such provision was exhausted; or

   (ii) was not under such a provision and either the coverage was terminated as a result of loss of eligibility for the coverage (including as a result of legal separation, divorce, death, termination of employment, or reduction in the number of hours of employment) or employer contributions toward such coverage were terminated.

(D) Under the terms of the plan, the employee requests such enrollment not later than 30 days after the date of exhaustion of coverage described in subparagraph (C)(i) or termination of coverage or employer contribution described in subparagraph (C)(ii).

(2) For dependent beneficiaries.

   (A) In general. If—

      (i) a group health plan makes coverage available with respect to a dependent of an individual,

(ii) the individual is a participant under the plan (or has met any waiting period applicable to becoming a participant under the plan and is eligible to be enrolled under the plan but for a failure to enroll during a previous enrollment period), and

(iii) a person becomes such a dependent of the individual through marriage, birth, or adoption or placement for adoption,

the group health plan shall provide for a dependent special enrollment period described in subparagraph (B) during which the person (or, if not otherwise enrolled, the individual) may be enrolled under the plan as a dependent of the individual, and in the case of the birth or adoption of a child, the spouse of the individual may be enrolled as a dependent of the individual if such spouse is otherwise eligible for coverage.

(B) Dependent special enrollment period. A dependent special enrollment period under this subparagraph shall be a period of not less than 30 days and shall begin on the later of—

(i) the date dependent coverage is made available, or

(ii) the date of the marriage, birth, or adoption or placement for adoption (as the case may be) described in subparagraph (A)(iii).

(C) No waiting period. If an individual seeks to enroll a dependent during the first 30 days of such a dependent special enrollment period, the coverage of the dependent shall become effective—

(i) in the case of marriage, not later than the first day of the first month beginning after the date the completed request for enrollment is received;

(ii) in the case of a dependent's birth, as of the date of such birth; or

(iii) in the case of a dependent's adoption or placement for adoption, the date of such adoption or placement for adoption.

(g) Use of affiliation period by HMOs as alternative to preexisting condition exclusion.

(1) In general. A health maintenance organization which offers health insurance coverage in connection with a group health plan and which does not impose any preexisting condition exclusion allowed under subsection (a) with respect to any particular coverage option may impose an affiliation period for such coverage option, but only if—

(A) such period is applied uniformly without regard to any health status-related factors; and

(B) such period does not exceed 2 months (or 3 months in the case of a late enrollee).

(2) Affiliation period.

(A) Defined. For purposes of this title, the term "affiliation period" means a period which, under the terms of the health insurance coverage offered by the health maintenance organization, must expire before the health insurance coverage becomes effective. The organization is not required to provide health care services or benefits during such period and no premium shall be charged to the participant or beneficiary for any coverage during the period.

(B) Beginning. Such period shall begin on the enrollment date.

(C) Runs concurrently with waiting periods. An affiliation period under a plan shall run concurrently with any waiting period under the plan.

(3) Alternative methods. A health maintenance organization described in paragraph (1) may use alternative methods, from those described in such paragraph, to address adverse selection as approved by the State insurance commissioner or official or officials designated by the State to enforce the requirements of this part for the State involved with respect to such issuer.

42 U.S.C. § 300gg-1. Prohibiting discrimination against individual participants and beneficiaries based on health status.

(a) In eligibility to enroll.

   (1) In general. Subject to paragraph (2), a group health plan, and a health insurance issuer offering group health insurance coverage in connection with a group health plan, may not establish rules for eligibility (including continued eligibility) of any individual to enroll under the terms of the plan based on any of the following health status-related factors in relation to the individual or a dependent of the individual:

      (A) Health status.
      (B) Medical condition (including both physical and mental illnesses).
      (C) Claims experience.
      (D) Receipt of health care.
      (E) Medical history.
      (F) Genetic information.
      (G) Evidence of insurability (including conditions arising out of acts of domestic violence).
      (H) Disability.

   (2) No application to benefits or exclusions. To the extent consistent with section 701, paragraph (1) shall not be construed—

      (A) to require a group health plan, or group health insurance coverage, to provide particular benefits other than those provided under the terms of such plan or coverage, or
      (B) to prevent such a plan or coverage from establishing limitations or restrictions on the amount, level, extent, or nature of the benefits or coverage for similarly situated individuals enrolled in the plan or coverage.

   (3) Construction. For purposes of paragraph (1), rules for eligibility to enroll under a plan include rules defining any applicable waiting periods for such enrollment.

(b) In premium contributions.

   (1) In general. A group health plan, and a health insurance issuer offering health insurance coverage in con-

nection with a group health plan, may not require any individual (as a condition of enrollment or continued enrollment under the plan) to pay a premium or contribution which is greater than such premium or contribution for a similarly situated individual enrolled in the plan on the basis of any health status-related factor in relation to the individual or to an individual enrolled under the plan as a dependent of the individual.

(2) Construction. Nothing in paragraph (1) shall be construed—

(A) to restrict the amount that an employer may be charged for coverage under a group health plan; or

(B) to prevent a group health plan, and a health insurance issuer offering group health insurance coverage, from establishing premium discounts or rebates or modifying otherwise applicable copayments or deductibles in return for adherence to programs of health promotion and disease prevention.

Appendix B

Mental Health Benefit Parity Act

29 U.S.C. § 1185A. Parity in the application of certain limits to mental health benefits

(a) In general.

  (1) Aggregate lifetime limits. In the case of a group health plan (or health insurance coverage offered in connection with such a plan) that provides both medical and surgical benefits and mental health benefits—

    (A) No lifetime limit. If the plan or coverage does not include an aggregate lifetime limit on substantially all medical and surgical benefits, the plan or coverage may not impose any aggregate lifetime limit on mental health benefits.

    (B) Lifetime limit. If the plan or coverage includes an aggregate lifetime limit on substantially all medical and surgical benefits (in this paragraph referred to as the "applicable lifetime limit"), the plan or coverage shall either—

      (i) apply the applicable lifetime limit both to the medical and surgical benefits to which it otherwise would apply and to mental health benefits and not distinguish in the application of such limit between such medical and surgical benefits and mental health benefits; or

(ii) not include any aggregate lifetime limit on mental health benefits that is less than the applicable lifetime limit.

(C) Rule in case of different limits. In the case of a plan or coverage that is not described in subparagraph (A) or (B) and that includes no or different aggregate lifetime limits on different categories of medical and surgical benefits, the Secretary shall establish rules under which subparagraph (B) is applied to such plan or coverage with respect to mental health benefits by substituting for the applicable lifetime limit an average aggregate lifetime limit that is computed taking into account the weighted average of the aggregate lifetime limits applicable to such categories.

(2) Annual limits. In the case of a group health plan (or health insurance coverage offered in connection with such a plan) that provides both medical and surgical benefits and mental health benefits—

(A) No annual limit. If the plan or coverage does not include an annual limit on substantially all medical and surgical benefits, the plan or coverage may not impose any annual limit on mental health benefits.

(B) Annual limit. If the plan or coverage includes an annual limit on substantially all medical and surgical benefits (in this paragraph referred to as the "applicable annual limit"), the plan or coverage shall either—

(i) apply the applicable annual limit both to medical and surgical benefits to which it otherwise would apply and to mental health benefits and not distinguish in the application of such limit between such medical and surgical benefits and mental health benefits; or

(ii) not include any annual limit on mental health benefits that is less than the applicable annual limit.

(C) Rule in case of different limits. In the case of a plan or coverage that is not described in subparagraph (A) or (B) and that includes no or different annual limits on different categories of medical and surgical benefits, the Secretary shall establish rules under which subparagraph (B) is applied to such plan or coverage with respect to mental health benefits by substituting for the applicable annual limit an average annual limit that is computed taking into account the weighted average of the annual limits applicable to such categories.

(b) Construction. Nothing in this section shall be construed—

(1) as requiring a group health plan (or health insurance coverage offered in connection with such a plan) to provide any mental health benefits; or

(2) in the case of a group health plan (or health insurance coverage offered in connection with such a plan) that provides mental health benefits, as affecting the terms and conditions (including cost sharing, limits on numbers of visits or days of coverage, and requirements relating to medical necessity) relating to the amount, duration, or scope of mental health benefits under the plan or coverage, except as specifically provided in subsection (a) (in regard to parity in the imposition of aggregate lifetime limits and annual limits for mental health benefits).

(c) Exemptions.

(1) Small employer exemption.

(A) In general. This section shall not apply to any group health plan (and group health insurance coverage offered in connection with a group health plan) for any plan year of a small employer.

(B) Small employer. For purposes of subparagraph (A), the term "small employer" means, in connection with a group health plan with respect to a calendar year and a plan year, an employer who employed an average of at least 2 but not more than 50 employees on business days during the preceding calendar year and who employs at least 2 employees on the first day of the plan year.

(C) Application of certain rules in determination of employer size. For purposes of this paragraph—

(i) Application of aggregation rule for employers. Rules similar to the rules under subsections (b), (c), (m), and (o) of section 414 of the Internal Revenue Code of 1986 shall apply for purposes of treating persons as a single employer.

(ii) Employers not in existence in preceding year. In the case of an employer which was not in existence throughout the preceding calendar year, the determination of whether such employer is a small employer shall be based on the average number of employees that it is reasonably expected such employer will employ on business days in the current calendar year.

(iii) Predecessors. Any reference in this paragraph to an employer shall include a reference to any predecessor of such employer.

(2) Increased cost exemption. This section shall not apply with respect to a group health plan (or health insurance coverage offered in connection with a group health plan) if the application of this section to such plan (or to such coverage) results in an increase in the cost under the plan (or for such coverage) of at least 1 percent.

(d) Separate application to each option offered. In the case of a group health plan that offers a participant or beneficiary two or more benefit package options under the plan, the requirements of this section shall be applied separately with respect to each such option.

(e) Definitions. For purposes of this section—

(1) Aggregate lifetime limit. The term "aggregate lifetime limit" means, with respect to benefits under a group health plan or health insurance coverage, a dollar limitation on the total amount that may be paid with re-

spect to such benefits under the plan or health insurance coverage with respect to an individual or other coverage unit.

(2) Annual limit. The term "annual limit" means, with respect to benefits under a group health plan or health insurance coverage, a dollar limitation on the total amount of benefits that may be paid with respect to such benefits in a 12-month period under the plan or health insurance coverage with respect to an individual or other coverage unit.

(3) Medical or surgical benefits. The term "medical or surgical benefits" means benefits with respect to medical or surgical services, as defined under the terms of the plan or coverage (as the case may be), but does not include mental health benefits.

(4) Mental health benefits. The term "mental health benefits" means benefits with respect to mental health services, as defined under the terms of the plan or coverage (as the case may be), but does not include benefits with respect to treatment of substance abuse or chemical dependency.

(f) Sunset. This section shall not apply to benefits for services furnished on or after September 30, 2001.

Appendix C

The Newborns' and Mothers' Health Protection Act

29 U.S.C. § 1185. Standards relating to benefits for mothers and newborns

(a) Requirements for minimum hospital stay following birth.

  (1) In general. A group health plan, and a health insurance issuer offering group health insurance coverage, may not—

    (A) except as provided in paragraph (2)—

      (i) restrict benefits for any hospital length of stay in connection with childbirth for the mother or newborn child, following a normal vaginal delivery, to less than 48 hours, or

      (ii) restrict benefits for any hospital length of stay in connection with childbirth for the mother or newborn child, following a cesarean section, to less than 96 hours; or

    (B) require that a provider obtain authorization from the plan or the issuer for prescribing any length of stay required under subparagraph (A) (without regard to paragraph (2)).

  (2) Exception. Paragraph (1)(A) shall not apply in connection with any group health plan or health insurance issuer in any case in which the decision to discharge the mother or her newborn child prior to the expiration of the minimum length of stay otherwise re-

quired under paragraph (1)(A) is made by an attending provider in consultation with the mother.

(b) Prohibitions. A group health plan, and a health insurance issuer offering group health insurance coverage in connection with a group health plan, may not—
   (1) deny to the mother or her newborn child eligibility, or continued eligibility, to enroll or to renew coverage under the terms of the plan, solely for the purpose of avoiding the requirements of this section;
   (2) provide monetary payments or rebates to mothers to encourage such mothers to accept less than the minimum protections available under this section;
   (3) penalize or otherwise reduce or limit the reimbursement of an attending provider because such provider provided care to an individual participant or beneficiary in accordance with this section;
   (4) provide incentives (monetary or otherwise) to an attending provider to induce such provider to provide care to an individual participant or beneficiary in a manner inconsistent with this section; or
   (5) subject to subsection (c)(3), restrict benefits for any portion of a period within a hospital length of stay required under subsection (a) in a manner which is less favorable than the benefits provided for any preceding portion of such stay.

(c) Rules of construction.
   (1) Nothing in this section shall be construed to require a mother who is a participant or beneficiary—
      (A) to give birth in a hospital; or
      (B) to stay in the hospital for a fixed period of time following the birth of her child.
   (2) This section shall not apply with respect to any group health plan, or any group health insurance coverage offered by a health insurance issuer, which does not provide benefits for hospital lengths of stay in connection with childbirth for a mother or her newborn child.
   (3) Nothing in this section shall be construed as preventing a group health plan or issuer from imposing de-

ductibles, coinsurance, or other cost-sharing in relation to benefits for hospital lengths of stay in connection with childbirth for a mother or newborn child under the plan (or under health insurance coverage offered in connection with a group health plan), except that such coinsurance or other cost-sharing for any portion of a period within a hospital length of stay required under subsection (a) may not be greater than such coinsurance or cost-sharing for any preceding portion of such stay.

(d) Notice under group health plan. The imposition of the requirements of this section shall be treated as a material modification in the terms of the plan described in section 102(a)(1), for purposes of assuring notice of such requirements under the plan; except that the summary description required to be provided under the last sentence of section 104(b)(1) with respect to such modification shall be provided by not later than 60 days after the first day of the first plan year in which such requirements apply.

(e) Level and type of reimbursements. Nothing in this section shall be construed to prevent a group health plan or a health insurance issuer offering group health insurance coverage from negotiating the level and type of reimbursement with a provider for care provided in accordance with this section.

(f) Preemption; exception for health insurance coverage in certain States.

  (1) In general. The requirements of this section shall not apply with respect to health insurance coverage if there is a State law (as defined in section 731 (d)(1)) for a State that regulates such coverage that is described in any of the following subparagraphs:

    (A) Such State law requires such coverage to provide for at least a 48-hour hospital length of stay following a normal vaginal delivery and at least a 96-hour hospital length of stay following a cesarean section.

    (B) Such State law requires such coverage to provide for maternity and pediatric care in accordance with guidelines established by the American College of Obstetricians and Gynecologists, the American Academy of Pediatrics, or other established professional medical associations.

(C) Such State law requires, in connection with such coverage for maternity care, that the hospital length of stay for such care is left to the decision of (or required to be made by) the attending provider in consultation with the mother.

(2) Construction. Section 731(a)(1) shall not be construed as superseding a State law described in paragraph (1).

42 U.S.C. § 300gg-4. Standards relating to benefits for mothers and newborns

(a) Requirements for minimum hospital stay following birth.

(1) In general. A group health plan, and a health insurance issuer offering group health insurance coverage, may not—

(A) except as provided in paragraph (2)—

(i) restrict benefits for any hospital length of stay in connection with childbirth for the mother or newborn child, following a normal vaginal delivery, to less than 48 hours, or

(ii) restrict benefits for any hospital length of stay in connection with childbirth for the mother or newborn child, following a cesarean section, to less than 96 hours, or

(B) require that a provider obtain authorization from the plan or the issuer for prescribing any length of stay required under subparagraph (A) (without regard to paragraph (2)).

(2) Exception. Paragraph (1)(A) shall not apply in connection with any group health plan or health insurance issuer in any case in which the decision to discharge the mother or her newborn child prior to the expiration of the minimum length of stay otherwise required under paragraph (1)(A) is made by an attending provider in consultation with the mother.

(b) Prohibitions. A group health plan, and a health insurance issuer offering group health insurance coverage in connection with a group health plan, may not—

(1) deny to the mother or her newborn child eligibility, or continued eligibility, to enroll or to renew coverage under the terms of the plan, solely for the purpose of avoiding the requirements of this section;

(2) provide monetary payments or rebates to mothers to encourage such mothers to accept less than the minimum protections available under this section;

(3) penalize or otherwise reduce or limit the reimbursement of an attending provider because such provider provided care to an individual participant or beneficiary in accordance with this section;

(4) provide incentives (monetary or otherwise) to an attending provider to induce such provider to provide care to an individual participant or beneficiary in a manner inconsistent with this section; or

(5) subject to subsection (c)(3), restrict benefits for any portion of a period within a hospital length of stay required under subsection (a) in a manner which is less favorable than the benefits provided for any preceding portion of such stay.

(c) Rules of construction.

(1) Nothing in this section shall be construed to require a mother who is a participant or beneficiary—

(A) to give birth in a hospital; or

(B) to stay in the hospital for a fixed period of time following the birth of her child.

(2) This section shall not apply with respect to any group health plan, or any group health insurance coverage offered by a health insurance issuer, which does not provide benefits for hospital lengths of stay in connection with childbirth for a mother or her newborn child.

(3) Nothing in this section shall be construed as preventing a group health plan or issuer from imposing deductibles, coinsurance, or other cost-sharing in relation to benefits for hospital lengths of stay in connec-

tion with childbirth for a mother or newborn child under the plan (or under health insurance coverage offered in connection with a group health plan), except that such coinsurance or other cost-sharing for any portion of a period within a hospital length of stay required under subsection (a) may not be greater than such coinsurance or cost-sharing for any preceding portion of such stay.

(d) Notice. A group health plan under this part shall comply with the notice requirement under section 711(d) of the Employee Retirement Income Security Act of 1974 with respect to the requirements of this section as if such section applied to such plan.

(e) Level and type of reimbursements. Nothing in this section shall be construed to prevent a group health plan or a health insurance issuer offering group health insurance coverage from negotiating the level and type of reimbursement with a provider for care provided in accordance with this section.

(f) Preemption; exception for health insurance coverage in certain States.

(1) In general. The requirements of this section shall not apply with respect to health insurance coverage if there is a State law (as defined in section 2723(d)(1)) for a State that regulates such coverage that is described in any of the following subparagraphs:

(A) Such State law requires such coverage to provide for at least a 48-hour hospital length of stay following a normal vaginal delivery and at least a 96-hour hospital length of stay following a cesarean section.

(B) Such State law requires such coverage to provide for maternity and pediatric care in accordance with guidelines established by the American College of Obstetricians and Gynecologists, the American Academy of Pediatrics, or other established professional medical associations.

(C) Such State law requires, in connection with such coverage for maternity care, that the hospital length of stay for such care is left to the decision of (or required to be made by) the attending provider in consultation with the mother.

(2) Construction. Section 2723(a)(1) shall not be construed as superseding a State law described in paragraph (1).

42 U.S.C. § 300gg-5. Parity in the application of certain limits to mental health benefits

(a) In general.

(1) Aggregate lifetime limits. In the case of a group health plan (or health insurance coverage offered in connection with such a plan) that provides both medical and surgical benefits and mental health benefits—

(A) No lifetime limit. If the plan or coverage does not include an aggregate lifetime limit on substantially all medical and surgical benefits, the plan or coverage may not impose any aggregate lifetime limit on mental health benefits.

(B) Lifetime limit. If the plan or coverage includes an aggregate lifetime limit on substantially all medical and surgical benefits (in this paragraph referred to as the "applicable lifetime limit"), the plan or coverage shall either—

(i) apply the applicable lifetime limit both to the medical and surgical benefits to which it otherwise would apply and to mental health benefits and not distinguish in the application of such limit between such medical and surgical benefits and mental health benefits; or

(ii) not include any aggregate lifetime limit on mental health benefits that is less than the applicable lifetime limit.

(C) Rule in case of different limits. In the case of a plan or coverage that is not described in subparagraph (A) or (B) and that includes no or different aggregate lifetime limits on different categories of medical and surgical benefits, the Secretary shall establish rules under which subparagraph (B) is applied to such plan or coverage with respect to mental health benefits by substituting for the applicable lifetime limit an average aggregate lifetime limit that is computed taking into account the weighted average of the aggregate lifetime limits applicable to such categories.

(2) Annual limits. In the case of a group health plan (or health insurance coverage offered in connection with such a plan) that provides both medical and surgical benefits and mental health benefits—
   (A) No annual limit. If the plan or coverage does not include an annual limit on substantially all medical and surgical benefits, the plan or coverage may not impose any annual limit on mental health benefits.
   (B) Annual limit. If the plan or coverage includes an annual limit on substantially all medical and surgical benefits (in this paragraph referred to as the "applicable annual limit"), the plan or coverage shall either—
      (i) apply the applicable annual limit both to medical and surgical benefits to which it otherwise would apply and to mental health benefits and not distinguish in the application of such limit between such medical and surgical benefits and mental health benefits; or
      (ii) not include any annual limit on mental health benefits that is less than the applicable annual limit.
   (C) Rule in case of different limits. In the case of a plan or coverage that is not described in subparagraph (A) or (B) and that includes no or different annual limits on different categories of medical and surgical benefits, the Secretary shall establish rules under which subparagraph (B) is applied to such plan or coverage with respect to mental health benefits by substituting for the applicable

annual limit an average annual limit that is computed taking into account the weighted average of the annual limits applicable to such categories.

(b) Construction. Nothing in this section shall be construed—
   (1) as requiring a group health plan (or health insurance coverage offered in connection with such a plan) to provide any mental health benefits; or
   (2) in the case of a group health plan (or health insurance coverage offered in connection with such a plan) that provides mental health benefits, as affecting the terms and conditions (including cost sharing, limits on numbers of visits or days of coverage, and requirements relating to medical necessity) relating to the amount, duration, or scope of mental health benefits under the plan or coverage, except as specifically provided in subsection (a) (in regard to parity in the imposition of aggregate lifetime limits and annual limits for mental health benefits).

(c) Exemptions.
   (1) Small employer exemption. This section shall not apply to any group health plan (and group health insurance coverage offered in connection with a group health plan) for any plan year of a small employer.
   (2) Increased cost exemption. This section shall not apply with respect to a group health plan (or health insurance coverage offered in connection with a group health plan) if the application of this section to such plan (or to such coverage) results in an increase in the cost under the plan (or for such coverage) of at least 1 percent.

(d) Separate application to each option offered. In the case of a group health plan that offers a participant or beneficiary two or more benefit package options under the plan, the requirements of this section shall be applied separately with respect to each such option.

(e) Definitions. For purposes of this section—
   (1) Aggregate lifetime limit. The term "aggregate lifetime limit" means, with respect to benefits under a group health plan or health insurance coverage, a dollar lim-

itation on the total amount that may be paid with respect to such benefits under the plan or health insurance coverage with respect to an individual or other coverage unit.

(2) Annual limit. The term "annual limit" means, with respect to benefits under a group health plan or health insurance coverage, a dollar limitation on the total amount of benefits that may be paid with respect to such benefits in a 12-month period under the plan or health insurance coverage with respect to an individual or other coverage unit.

(3) Medical or surgical benefits. The term "medical or surgical benefits" means benefits with respect to medical or surgical services, as defined under the terms of the plan or coverage (as the case may be), but does not include mental health benefits.

(4) Mental health benefits. The term "mental health benefits" means benefits with respect to mental health services, as defined under the terms of the plan or coverage (as the case may be), but does not include benefits with respect to treatment of substance abuse or chemical dependency.

(f) Sunset. This section shall not apply to benefits for services furnished on or after September 30, 2001.

42 U.S.C. § 300gg-51. Standards relating to benefits for mothers and newborns

(a) In general. The provisions of section 2704 (other than subsections (d) and (f)) shall apply to health insurance coverage offered by a health insurance issuer in the individual market in the same manner as it applies to health insurance coverage offered by a health insurance issuer in connection with a group health plan in the small or large group market.

(b) Notice requirement. A health insurance issuer under this part shall comply with the notice requirement under section 711(d) of the Employee Retirement Income Security Act of 1974 with respect to the requirements referred to in subsection (a) as if such section applied to such issuer and such issuer were a group health plan.

(c) Preemption; exception for health insurance coverage in certain States.

 (1) In general. The requirements of this section shall not apply with respect to health insurance coverage if there is a State law (as defined in section 2723(d)(1)) for a State that regulates such coverage that is described in any of the following subparagraphs:

  (A) Such State law requires such coverage to provide for at least a 48-hour hospital length of stay following a normal vaginal delivery and at least a 96-hour hospital length of stay following a cesarean section.

  (B) Such State law requires such coverage to provide for maternity and pediatric care in accordance with guidelines established by the American College of Obstetricians and Gynecologists, the American Academy of Pediatrics, or other established professional medical associations.

  (C) Such State law requires, in connection with such coverage for maternity care, that the hospital length of stay for such care is left to the decision of (or required to be made by) the attending provider in consultation with the mother.

 (2) Construction. Section 2762(a) shall not be construed as superseding a State law described in paragraph (1).

Index

D

E

F

I

L

M

N

O

P

9 780834 211582

Printed in Dunstable, United Kingdom

88190711R00070